THE MANY FACES OF SCHOOL LIBRARY LEADERSHIP

D1311628

Sharon Coatney, Editor

LIBRARIES UNLIMITED

AN IMPRINT OF ABC-CLIO, LLC
Santa Barbara, California • Denver, Colorado • Oxford, England

Library of Congress Cataloging-in-Publication Data

The many faces of school library leadership / Sharon Coatney, editor.
   p. cm.
  Includes bibliographical references and index.
   ISBN 978–1–59158–893–1 (acid-free paper) — ISBN 978–1–59158–894–8 (ebook)
   1. School libraries—United States—Administration. 2. Instructional materials centers—United States—
Administration. 3. School librarian participation in curriculum planning. 4. Teacher-librarians. 5. Leadership. I. Coatney, Sharon.
Z675.S3M36   2010
025.1'978—dc22   2010002031

ISBN: 978–1–59158–893–1
EISBN: 978–1–59158–894–8

14 13 12 11 10   1 2 3 4 5

This book is also available on the World Wide Web as an eBook.
Visit www.abc-clio.com for details.

Libraries Unlimited
An Imprint of ABC-CLIO, LLC

ABC-CLIO, LLC
130 Cremona Drive, P.O. Box 1911
Santa Barbara, California 93116-1911

This book is printed on acid-free paper ∞

Manufactured in the United States of America

To Ruth Bell, former Director of Library Media Services, Blue Valley School District, Overland Park, Kansas; twice winner of the AASL National School Library Media Program of the Year Award for exemplary library programs at the district level; inspirational leader and visionary professional.

Contents

Introduction

Sharon Coatney

Being a school librarian, a teacher-librarian, a school library media specialist, a library media specialist, a library teacher is a difficult, many-faceted job but a wonderful one as well. The essays in this volume, written by leaders and thinkers in the field (practitioners and library educators), are a thoughtful look at a job that is very big, that is not universally defined in the same manner, and that can be very rewarding.

Throughout the book, the terminology is fluid, as essayists from different perspectives use the term to identify the job with which they are the most comfortable. This lack of a common name in itself indicates the problem of defining just what the job is; however, the common goal of effecting student achievement does define the job—no matter what we call ourselves.

In 1988, the American Association of School Librarians (AASL) said,

The mission of the library media program is to ensure that students and staff are effective users of ideas and information. (American Association of School Librarians and Association for Educational Communications and Technology 1988)

This mission was reconfirmed in 1998 with the publication of *Information Power: Building Partnerships for Learning* (AASL and Association for Educational Communications and Technology, 1998) and reconfirmed again and expanded in 2009 to say:

The mission of the school library media program is to ensure that students and staff are effective users of ideas and information. The school library media specialist empowers students to be critical thinkers, enthusiastic readers, skillful researchers and ethical users of ideas and information. (AASL 2009)

We, as professionals, agree to the mission and acknowledge that the way to accomplish it is through exercising leadership:

providing leadership in the total education program and advocating for strong school library media programs as essential to meeting local, state, and national education goals. (AASL 2009)

Being accepted as a leader in one's school is not an easy or automatic outcome of accepting a position for which leadership is a recommended function. School librarians need to know where they are going in order to lead, long before they think about how to do it. Knowing, defining, and, more importantly, agreeing with the underlying belief and mission of the school in which one has accepted a position is the bottom line.

The bottom line is this: library media specialists must see their work as "the school's work" not just because the physical space and resources are shared by all, but because the significance of the learning that is conducted in the library media center is at the heart of the school's purpose. (Zmuda and Harada 2008)

Once agreement with the mission is established, the work begins. School library media specialists are uniquely placed to be instructional leaders and to support the instructional mission of the school. They have the training (as teachers themselves) and the professional goals and skills as librarians to aid teachers in accomplishing the goal of increasing student achievement. Their leadership role is multifaceted, and an accomplished school library media specialist will be able to provide leadership and to effect the instruction of the school and the achievement of students over time by:

- Keeping current on the research into best instructional practices and providing information and training for faculty and staff—thus encouraging best practice and promoting student achievement.
- Keeping up-to-date on current technologies and providing training for faculty and staff—thus encouraging student motivation, interest, and innovation.
- Serving on curriculum committees and providing leadership to integrate student inquiry into the school's curriculum—thus encouraging best practice and promoting student achievement.
- Keeping abreast of current literature for children and young adults and promoting the love of reading through programs and activities to encourage reading for pleasure—thus promoting student achievement.
- Modeling best practice in instruction and innovative uses of technology, teaching students the skills necessary to structure inquiry while fostering the disposition of lifelong learning—thus promoting best practice.
- Helping teachers teach—thus promoting and modeling best practice, encouraging trust, and fostering student achievement.
- Modeling and promoting privacy, ethical use of information, equal access to information, and intellectual freedom by informing students, staff, and faculty of accepted practices and legal and ethical requirements—thus promoting trust and enhancing and empowering students' access to all information.
- Envisioning the future and always looking for new and better ways to promote student inquiry and build a more effective learning community.

The essayists will discuss all facets of school library leadership. Ken Haycock discusses the big picture of leadership—what it is and how we can prepare personally to become effective leaders. Violet Harada describes our function as the "learning leader," a critical component in our schools. In the third chapter, Deb Levitov, a well-known expert on advocacy, reminds us of our responsibility to lead as advocates for our school library programs in order to promote student learning. Helen Adams looks at the critical need for leadership in the areas of intellectual freedom and privacy—key issues for school libraries. Doug Achterman, Jody Howard, and Kristin Fontichiaro look at leadership in the areas of literacy, curriculum, and technology. Janice Gilmore-See calls us to leadership in the area of staff development, and Blanche Woolls reminds us of our responsibility to others in our field—through leadership in our local, state, and national organizations. The book ends with a clarion call sounding the importance of visionary leadership, as David Loertscher challenges us to lead our schools and school libraries into the twenty-first century.

Each of us has strengths and weaknesses, things we enjoy doing more than others—but our learners need us to exercise leadership in all of these areas. We must become lifelong learners ourselves and continue to develop skills in the things we already do well, along with perhaps concentrating specifically on the things we do not do as well. Perhaps technology is a great personal strength. That is a very good thing, but one must remember to develop expertise as a curricular leader and literacy leader as well. Our students need all of these things from us. The key to becoming leaders in our schools is within each of us. Just like our students, school librarians need to cultivate and develop the dispositions, responsibilities, and skills necessary to become lifelong learners. As the old saying goes, we must "practice what we preach." A model is the best teacher.

The AASL's *Standards for the 21st-Century Learner* (2007) speaks to the learning needs of all ages. Learners are not just our students in grades pre-K–12. In any school building, there are many, many adults (staff, administrators, teachers, and parents) who can be encouraged and helped along the way toward lifelong learning by the presence, model, and active leadership of a school librarian who is a lifelong learner. By encouraging all of the adults in the building to model and demonstrate the disposition of a lifelong learner, we increase the number of models that our students see. Becoming that model for lifelong learning should be a goal of every school librarian. Developing and displaying the dispositions of curiosity, openness to new ideas, and motivation to seek information to answer personal questions is imperative (Coatney 2009).

Leadership, then, is a personal challenge for each of us as we strive to achieve the mission of the school library media program. School library leaders lead by example and by service. By constantly learning and updating our skills, we prepare ourselves to lead by example as excellent teachers, researchers, advocates, readers, collaborators, and users of technology—and in so doing we provide the excellent school library services needed to prepare students to live and work in the twenty-first century.

It is important to remember that school library leadership is from the middle. We are part of collaborative teaching and learning teams that work together to accomplish the mission of the school, using the expertise we have developed over time in all of the areas discussed in this book. We must assume the leadership of the learning team, and as such, we must remember these three guiding principles stated by North Carolina's award-winning basketball coach Roy Williams:

Everyone on the team must focus on the same goal. It is my job to effectively communicate those goals to the team. Emphasize those goals every day. Understand that although everyone has a common goal, individuals also have goals, needs and dreams that must be cared for. (Williams 2009)

Communicate, persevere, and remember to listen. The reward is student learning.

REFERENCES

American Association of School Librarians. 2009. *Empowering learners: Guidelines for school library media programs.* Chicago: American Association of School Librarians.

American Association of School Librarians and Association for Educational Communications and Technology. 1988. *Information power: Guidelines for school library media programs.* Chicago: American Library Association and Association for Educational Communications and Technology.

Coatney, Sharon. 2009. Opening the door to leadership—the key. *School Library Monthly* (December): 43–44.

Williams, Roy. 2009. Knowing leadership when you see it. *U.S. News and World Report* (November): 45.

Zmuda, Allison, and Violet H. Harada. *Librarians as learning specialists: Meeting the learning imperatives for the 21st century.* Westport, CT: Libraries Unlimited.

1

Leadership from the Middle: Building Influence for Change

Ken Haycock

Leadership remains an elusive yet critical component of school effectiveness. While many would suggest that leadership is easily recognized, this too often means that we appreciate managers who are simply behaving toward us and our particular interests and priorities in a way we like; we therefore label it "leadership." Most would concur that leadership and management are different. Michael Gorman writes,

> The essential differences between management/administration on the one hand and leadership on the other are that the former is concerned with what is and the latter is concerned with what will be. One accepts the *status quo* (and often yearns for the *status quo ante*) and the other dares to imagine and to create the future. (Gorman 1982)

Although the leadership literature naturally talks of leaders and followers, another role is to lead from the middle. When one leads from the middle, as teacher-librarians do, it is perhaps more appropriate to speak of leaders and colleagues.

Many theories and models of leadership (Chemers 1997) exist, and many of them are exhibited by school administrators, although they may not have been labeled. For many teacher-librarians, the most prized is transformational leadership, where they are working with administrators to develop a climate for change and a culture based on collaboration and mutual respect, and the least acceptable, "laissez-faire" leadership, where administrators do not intervene unless absolutely necessary.

Theories of leadership are complex and richly textured, with many different sub-theories and many different models for implementation. Following are some of the more common and well-researched theories relating to the role of the teacher-librarians and their relationships with principals, taken down to their bare essentials:

- *Attribution*, or how we assign causes to the interpersonal events that occur around us (some teacher-librarians are more successful in some types of schools than in others; some are more successful in certain school cultures than in others);

- *Contingency*, wherein leadership is primarily the exercise of social influence (where teacher-librarians recognize that influence is absolutely necessary to move colleagues to inquiry-based learning through collaboration);
- *Path-goal*, where motivation is influenced by the probability of certain behaviors leading to a specific and worthwhile goal (when the teacher-librarian develops relationships, influences behaviors, and develops patterns of collaboration, student achievement should be improved);
- *Performance-maintenance*, reaching goals while maintaining group stability (where teacher-librarians help colleagues to move forward to a culture of collaboration without unnecessary or unmanaged and unresolved conflict in the process);
- *Situational*, having the ability to balance both direction and support with the commitment and capability of others to undertake the task at hand (for the teacher-librarian, the planning process will look very different and be very different with the novice collaborator from with the experienced teaching partner);
- *Transactional*, where legitimacy rests on perceptions of competence and honesty, fairness and mutual loyalty (no one is going to invest time in working with someone who is not capable of adding value to the learning situation and committed to mutual success);
- *Transformational*, with self-confidence, and maintaining commitment to a vision, colleagues are more likely to meld their personal identity with that vision (a teacher-librarian exuding confidence, and committed to an integrated program based on trust and respect, is more likely to move colleagues to a shared vision without them feeling the loss of their individual and independent identities).

In fact, the successful teacher-librarian, working in concert with a like-minded school principal, will exhibit components of these theories and approaches at different times, in different contexts, and in different situations.

Just as there are many theories and models of leadership, so too there are many definitions; indeed, there are reportedly more than 300 definitions of leadership. So what is it exactly?

A definition that would be accepted by a majority of theorists and researchers would suggest that "leadership is a process of social influence in which one person is able to enlist the aid and support of others in the accomplishment of a common task" (Chemers 1997, 1). Leadership, then, is a group activity based on social influence. This supports the potential for "leadership from the middle"—that is, where the individual does not have position power but can exercise influence from a different position, similar to the role of the teacher-librarian. Obviously the common goal shared by all professionals in the school is student achievement and the quality of students' and teachers' experiences in the learning environment. How one addresses these goals, however, can vary considerably. The common task for the teacher-librarian is to develop this process of social influence, in which colleagues become committed to collaboration and instructional partnerships in order to enhance student learning.

If leadership is this social influence process of enlisting the aid and support of others in the accomplishment of a common task, a leader is consequently someone whom you would follow where you would not normally go alone, someone who rallies people to a better future.

LEADERSHIP IS ABOUT SPECIFIC COMPETENCIES

Leadership is a process, more than a role or position. For the teacher-librarian, this leadership is based on complex relationships of teacher, teacher-librarian, and school principal, in a changing environment resulting from differing priorities from the district and different levels of budgetary support from year to year.

Leadership is about the competence of a highly competent individual who is driven by a compelling vision, able to communicate that image of competence and trustworthiness, who understands deeply the political and learning environment and is able to mobilize resources to achieve success. Teacher-librarians are highly competent visionaries who understand the environment and lead in combining human and material resources to achieve learning objectives.

Bennis (1989) notes four specific core competencies for leaders: managing attention, managing meaning, managing trust, and managing oneself. According to Bennis, managing attention is the ability to communicate that extraordinary focus of commitment, to communicate a compelling vision in the context of goals and directions that others can galvanize their efforts behind. Staying centered on the ultimate goal, ensuring that the focus is on collaboration for student learning, helps to move the agenda forward.

What is our core strength and contribution to the school through the school library program? Is this valued? The answer to this question should relate to the competencies and roles played by the teacher-librarian, not simply the presence of resources. Why is a teacher-librarian fundamentally necessary in the school? Recognize that others can manage resources and facilities. If great leaders rally people to a better future, that future is part of the vision. The teacher-librarian manages attention on that vision, ensuring that the more mundane aspects of program administration or lower-level service priorities do not become the preferred outcome.

Managing meaning, that is, making dreams apparent to others, and communicating through meaningful models and examples ensures preferred futures and a roadmap to get there. What is that meaning? What is the vision for a strong, integrated school library program? Is there clarity to our vision? How will the program, and the players, look different in five years? What are the implications? What is a reasonable plan for progress?

It should be possible to answer some basic questions here. For example, whom do we serve? Most would answer students, yet the primary clientele in terms of power, impact, and effect would be teachers. How do we serve students better while working through their classroom teacher? What models do we present for improved collaboration and student learning that make the extra effort worthwhile? How do we "serve" without being subservient? How do we negotiate positions of equal partnership? The teacher-librarian manages meaning for the program by enabling each student to access and make effective use of information and ideas through collaborative program planning and teaching with classroom colleagues.

Managing trust involves the constancy of people knowing what you stand for and where you stand and the subsequent consistency of behaviors. There are no surprises. What is our "core score" as teacher-librarians? How are we doing? How do we know? What are our measures of success? Who agrees with these measures? Who are the partners in leadership and implementation? What role does the principal or superintendent play?

Managing oneself, knowing the extent of one's skills and applying them effectively, may be the most challenging competence of all. What actions can we take today? How do we collect and confront the "brutal facts" about our program, the degree of success in implementation and its positive effect on teachers and students? Are we able to take disciplined action to move the program forward? What do we need to know and be able to do in order to be successful? Studies in our own field demonstrate, for example, that teacher-librarians with education, training, and experience in collaboration are more likely to collaborate—competence leads to capability and confidence.

Regardless of preference of style or theory, however, a leader must be competent in the skills and abilities of leadership and able to maintain an extraordinary focus on what is important and what competencies, behaviors, and tasks will be necessary to move the organization forward. These responsibilities of leadership are consistent with the core competencies Bennis (1989) articulates:

- envisioning goals (you can actually picture them in practice);
- affirming values (you value mutual respect, collaboration, and partnerships);
- motivating (you are skilled at social influence and persuasion);
- managing (you are efficient and effective, recognizing the difference between the urgent and the important, delegating whatever is possible to delegate, even to student or parent/community volunteers).

Develop and demonstrate your competencies to be a powerful player in collaboration and inquiry. Show administrators and teachers what you are not good at and, in the collaborative process, try to lead others to do what they are more competent to do, especially when it is something that you do not do as well. Work with your principal to establish priorities.

LEADERSHIP IS ABOUT SPECIFIC BEHAVIORS

Leadership is essentially the ability to guide, direct, or influence people. Effective leadership then involves three major functions (Chemers 1997):

- *Image management*, the teacher-librarian's ability to project an image more than most colleagues' expectations (every study of teacher expectations shows that they initially expect less than professional-level work from their teacher-librarian colleague). Teacher-librarians must motivate teachers to see them as an instructional partner.
- *Relationship development*, success in creating and sustaining motivated and competent colleagues; this means being able to bring ideas to the fore, being confident and capable enough to inspire confidence in one's ability, and engendering a sense of adventure in the work.
- *Resource utilization*, deploying the assets of both self and others (including student and adult volunteers) to accomplishing the mission, to ensuring that collaboration and leadership are priorities.

Chemers (1997) also suggests two factors that make a difference in leadership behaviors, (1) consideration—that is, open communication with colleagues, mutual trust and respect, and interpersonal warmth, coupled with (2) initiation of structure—to organize and structure group activities, define relationships, and organize colleagues to task accomplishment. The former demands respect for the classroom teacher's world and challenges, as well as respect for his or her expertise, ability, and potential contributions. The latter suggests the need for greater scaffolding for the planning process, ensuring strong support for success and good questioning ability around partnerships and instructional goals; this is why a planning guide proves so useful, with indications of information needed by both partners and support required from each of the partners for implementation of the unit of study.

Successful leaders are skilled at group goal facilitation, able to move the group forward to accomplishing a task; at group sociability, able to interact socially and to effectively gain acceptance as a colleague and partner; and at individual prominence, having behaviors to make him or her stand out, with a distinct contribution. When working to motivate colleagues, teacher-librarians must believe that their efforts will be accepted, that the challenge will be worthwhile, and that eventually they will be successful. This applies as well to working with school principals, developing a working partnership, making that unique contribution known, managing expectations—in other words, "managing up."

Confidence in offering guidance and in motivating others, each handled with sensitivity, flexibility, and creativity, is required. Teacher-librarians can introduce new ideas to staff members, teachers, or principals if they are perceived to have competence and if they are seen as loyal to the group.

To successful teacher-librarians who enjoy the support of administrators and colleagues in encouraging inquiry-based learning in collaborative work environments, it will be no surprise that the appropriate behaviors for leadership come down to influence, persuasion, and negotiation. Leadership influences people to follow. Persuasion allows the teacher-librarian to convince others to join the effort, and negotiation means the teacher-librarian, through discussion, overcomes negative issues.

LEADERSHIP IS ABOUT RELATIONSHIPS

Leadership requires strong relationships. Indeed, the core of teacher-librarianship—collaboration and partnerships—rests on positive and productive relationships with colleagues and other staff. These relationships involve complex and strategic alliances, partnerships, and professional friendships on many levels.

At one level the foundations for workplace relationships are no different from those in our personal lives. They require trust and consistency in our actions, moral character, and mutual respect.

At another level, however, productive leader relationships are fostered through being able to motivate with an inspiring and understood vision and with deep concern for colleagues.

Teacher-librarians can communicate the potential of strong relationships through ideas and a sense of adventure. They must communicate, often and well, their respect for the work of others. In doing so, they will develop a strong communication network where they are the hub.

Teacher-librarians experienced in collaboration and school leadership will recognize the critical importance of relationships and the skills necessary to develop them. Those experienced in working in teams in schools and elsewhere will also recognize the behaviors and actions conducive to team development, as well as those that impair strong partnerships. According to Lencioni (2002, 2005), these specific tendencies enable teams: the presence of trust (this speaks to the core of mutual respect); the ability to acknowledge and deal with conflict (conflict is unavoidable in collaborative environments; the issue is whether it is addressed and managed); commitment (lack of commitment is too often perceived as teachers' reluctance to partner but is just as often a teacher-librarian issue); a focus on accountability (demonstrating the ability to produce results and how this added effort will benefit teachers and students); and attention to results (documenting site-specific improvement and effect rather than pointing to results from other areas and other states).

LEADERSHIP IS ABOUT INFLUENCE

Regardless of a particular preferred theory or approach, leadership is clearly about influence. Enlisting the aid and support of others in the accomplishment of a common task requires influence, whether working with a principal to provide support for clerical and technical jobs or with an individual teacher or team of teachers to collaborate around a project to enhance student learning.

Too often we have seen influence as commensurate with power, but the two are separate. Blanchard (1994) articulated five main points of power:

- *Position Power*, where you manage people and resources through a collaborative relationship with the principal to help your teachers work collaboratively on school-wide curriculum and projects. Indeed, there is some position power ascribed to the teacher-librarian, through the managing of space and resources and the budget to keep up-to-date resources and a large contingent of volunteer help in the school.
- *Task Power*, often connected to the accomplishment of a particular objective, such as providing staff development for learning new databases.
- *Personal Power*, wherein the combination of your skills and abilities leads to incredible influence; examples would include your communication skills, "people skills," leadership skills, your character, passion, inspiration, and vision.
- *Relationship Power*, based on friendships, your understanding and empathy for colleagues' situations and circumstances, and reciprocity with a well-developed and understood "quid pro quo" approach.
- *Knowledge Power*, as your experience (such as in a variety of classroom levels and settings), education (such as advanced study in reading or technology tools), and specialized skill (such as in collaboration or integrating information fluencies) make you the go-to person when your knowledge is valued and seen as worthy of seeking out.

Power is the exercise of social influence, and this influence is at the core of leading from the middle. Unfortunately, developing influence has proven to be difficult for some to achieve and an area that proves elusive in our educational and professional development. What actually inhibits the development of influence? According to Patterson and others (2007), there are major barriers to overcome. These are primarily attitudinal and preparatory.

A first barrier is the view that "it is not my job." This is a primary problem for those who do not believe that they should have to develop patterns of influence because they are a social and educational "good" and should be supported as such. Stated plainly, the world does not work this way anymore (if indeed it ever did). Too often, these same teacher-librarians are the first to decry cuts in staffing and resources without having done anything to forestall them. They have neglected even simple advocacy—a planned, deliberate, and systematic approach to developing understanding and support incrementally over time—advocacy, not publicity.

One area of concern is the confusion of advocacy (connecting agendas) with public relations or publicity (getting the message out). Talking is not influencing; talking is talking. It is important to know the "language" of the recipient(s) and their issues and concerns. (This may be one of many reasons why teacher-librarians with classroom experience tend to be more successful in engendering support—they anticipate instructional problems and understand the work world of colleagues.)

The second barrier to influence is the simple lack of a plan to enhance understanding and support. This failure to create a plan can be critical in some areas of teacher-librarian leadership, such as collaboration (the ability to deliver the goods through knowledge and expertise) or in the necessary skill areas for building influence. A useful and important exercise is to assess the degree of influence one already holds in a school or school district and build a plan to increase the understanding and support from your staff, teachers, and administrators. Many general and specialized resources exist for this activity (see, for example, Hartzell 2003 and Haycock 1990).

Simply stated, however, there is no silver bullet or quick fix. Building influence means building relationships and building trust, and those take time. Having a realistic plan, competence and consistency, and a deep understanding of effective practices will lead to enhanced roles over time.

One reason for having a plan is that you cannot try to influence everyone; there is neither the time nor the resources to do so. Instead, focus on opinion leaders in the building and district. These individuals should be well known to you through skilled observation and the development of informal sociograms to document communication patterns and power relationships among staff. We tend to rely too much on our own experience and introspection (what would motivate me?) rather than developing a plan based on evidence.

Recent studies suggest that there are six universal principles for becoming persuasive and developing influence (Goldstein, Martin, and Cialdini 2008). The suggestions provided here focus more on building influence with classroom teachers than on school principals and superintendents but apply equally well. While a strong partnership with the school principal is critical to the success of the teacher-librarian, at the same time, principals may tend to assess the teacher-librarian's performance based on the perceptions of classroom teachers rather than on direct experience.

- *Reciprocation.* We feel obliged to return favors performed for us. For teacher-librarians this becomes challenging, as we know that teachers initially see us in a subservient role rather than as an equal teaching partner, unless they have already had experience collaborating with a teacher-librarian. The result is that much of what we do is not a "favor" so much as merely our job and the teacher's due. This is certainly true of coverage of preparation or relief periods for classroom teachers. The question then becomes one of exceeding expectations (which are often low in any case) in a way that is particularly useful for a colleague at that particular time, whether offering resources or advice, working with a particular group, or assisting in the classroom. Principals see the offering of informal staff development and in-service programs by teacher-librarians as useful and effective in gaining stature in the school.
- *Authority.* We look to experts to show us the way. So, what is our expertise? It should exceed the classroom teacher's perceived expertise whether in resources (literature and technology tools) or services (collaboration and information fluencies). Expertise does not exist because we say it is so but rather as it is demonstrated. It takes little foundation to master a few steps in the information process (indeed we expect youngsters to do this); it takes much more to know a variety of models and the underlying skill and task sets necessary to build student and teacher competence and confidence. This expertise should then be easily and readily shared (Brown 1999) while building other areas of expertise.
- *Commitment and consistency.* We want to be reliable with our commitments and true to our values. One would hope that the school community as a whole is committed to learning, to quality experiences, and above all, to student achievement. It would be naïve to believe that this

is the case for every professional in the building, however. Similarly, teacher-librarians who focus on resources and strategies, while ignoring an individual teacher's belief system, are destined for problems. Some may appreciate and even admire the energies you expend, the expertise you bring, and the contributions you make, but their own values and beliefs about teaching and learning may not be aligned with resource-based learning and modes of inquiry.

- *Scarcity.* The less available the resource, the more we want it. But what is the resource? Is it children's books (which are often distributed throughout the school without a library)? Is it technological tools and access (which again can be available from any location)? Is it selected and indexed subscription databases (which most teachers consider to be free unless someone has disabused them)? Is it access to a facility or to expertise? Or is it a teaching partner? Which resource is most scarce and most valued in your environment? How do you leverage that scarcity for influence?
- *Liking.* The more we like people the more we want to say yes to them. Social relationships are part of any network. Building strong bonds, participating in school social events, and engaging with colleagues both in and out of school all contribute to being known and being liked. Individual preference in liking individual colleagues is somewhat irrelevant if you are committed to building a strong program. Relationships are the essence of leadership.
- *Social proof.* We look to what others do to guide our behaviors. Leadership involves change, and change involves working with opinion leaders. The more common collaboration becomes, the more it is accepted as a norm of behavior in the building and district. Stated another way, success breeds success. Identifying and working with teacher-leaders in the building and the district lead to greater influence and support.

ABOVE ALL, LEADERSHIP IS ABOUT YOU

While leadership theory focuses on specific means (such as influence) and the tasks, attributes, and skills to support those means, the bottom line is the individual leader and whether that individual can bring about the change sought.

The first person you manage and lead is, of course, yourself. It is important to organize yourself to be both efficient (this is necessary for survival and to allow you to give attention to what really matters) and effective (in order to be successful in achieving your programmatic goals).

There are many tools available to help you develop better understandings of yourself. One fairly common indicator used regularly in schools and school districts for understanding of type, temperament, and team development is the Myers-Briggs Type Indicator (MBTI). Sadly, the MBTI is often introduced at a staff development workshop for a day or even half-day with no follow-up or even reminders. The result is an interesting time but no long-term effect (but then this is common of many staff development programs).

"Type" is helpful in understanding yourself and other people. The MBTI reports some of your key preferences but certainly not all, and it does not look to stereotype or pigeonhole, only to develop understanding.

Only you can decide how accurate the report is for you.

There are four preference scales . . .

- *Extroversion or Introversion.* Do you get your energy from being around other people or being on your own? Is your life focused more externally or more internally? As with the other scales, a preference for extroversion does not mean that you do not like to spend time on your own, or the reverse. Extroverts may have a tendency to think and act or talk at the same time, while introverts think and then maybe act/talk. Successful leaders, including teacher-librarians, do exhibit the behaviors of extroverts, placing a premium on social interaction, time in the faculty lounge with colleagues, building relationships throughout the school. These behaviors can be learned. Although there are no right or wrong choices (hence the MBTI is an "indicator," not a test), many studies do show that successful leaders, and successful teacher-librarians, regardless of preference, do exhibit extroverted behaviors.

- *Sensing or Intuition.* Do you prefer to receive information through your five senses or through intuition? Do you have a preference for details or the big picture? Again, we can and should be skilled enough to focus on both but have a preference for one over the other; we also need to be mindful of our response to those who simply cannot see the big picture or who cannot focus on the necessary details. This has implications for collaborative planning, as some are very detail oriented while others take "broad brush" approaches to instructional decisions. As a teacher-librarian, you need to be able to recognize and deal with each. Knowing your own preference makes this easier.
- *Thinking or Feeling.* This is the only area where there is a gender difference, although it is not great. More men prefer to make decisions with their head, through logical analysis, while more women prefer to make decisions with their heart, based on values and group harmony.
- *Judgment or Perception.* And your interactions with the world? Are they planned and organized, or flexible and adaptable? These two preferences can also be at odds in a planning session . . .

Consider taking the Myers-Briggs Type Indicator through your employer or a not-for-profit agency. There are also online versions (typically adapted or condensed), but they are usually not as valid.

Once you know your MBTI type, then determine your leadership strengths and preferences (there are many resources to provide insights; see, for example, Myers 1998 for an introduction). You should also review the contributions that your MBTI type typically makes to a team or organization (see, for example, Hirsh and Kummerow 1998 and Kroeger, Thuesen, and Rutledge 2002). Of course, know too your potential pitfalls. From this assessment, you can develop objectives for your own development.

Another piece of this puzzle is identifying your specific organizational strengths. Over many years the Gallup Organization conducted research in thousands of organizations. They found that few of us are able to articulate our strengths. We can outline our qualifications and our experiences, and we can even point to some significant accomplishments, but we are not able to specify and articulate the underlying strengths that led to these actions. We are then hired due to the perception of our strengths but evaluated based on our weaknesses and told to correct those weaknesses. More and more research in strategic human relations management, however, is identifying the importance of hiring for talent/strengths and then encouraging the use and development of those strengths.

Beginning with *Now, Discover Your Strengths* (Buckingham and Clifton 2001), several approaches and contexts have been developed for "strengths-finding." Most provide a registration code in the book for an online assessment of your strengths. The Buckingham and Clifton assessment will provide you with your top 5 (of 34 possible) strengths, along with a description of each. The profile will also suggest ways that the strength is typically used successfully in organizations and how each might be developed. Identification of strengths is important for several reasons. First, it provides insight into your natural areas of interest and preference for development. Second, it helps you to determine whether your current work environment and position help you to work with your strengths (if not, you may find that this explains why you are unhappy in your position). Third, it allows you to soar, to really demonstrate what you can do.

Newer applications of using strengths have recently been developed—for specific examples, in teaching (Liesveld and Miller 2005) and in leadership (Rath and Conchie 2008). The domains of leadership strengths are not unlike those identified by other researchers: executing, influencing, relationship building, strategic thinking.

Knowing yourself allows you to build confidence in your abilities and strengths. Peter Drucker, perhaps the leading management guru of the past century, like other researchers and theorists, states that self-confidence is an absolute necessity for success (Cohen 2007). Drucker also notes that what "everybody" knows is frequently wrong and that we should approach problems with ignorance and an open mind. Interestingly, Drucker's research also found that executives should stay no longer than six years in the same position; perhaps the same might be said of any leader. It may comfort teacher-librarians to know that Drucker believes that some so-called menial tasks can only be done by the leader, such that everyone needs to be an effective manager as well as a leader.

There are some basic attributes of leadership (Gardner 1990). Added to the competencies, tasks, and skills discussed earlier, these round out the characteristics of the effective leader:

- physical vitality and stamina (especially as most of the key components of teacher-librarianship—planning, collaboration, resource allocation—take place outside of the school day);
- intelligence and judgment in action (knowing when to move forward and when to compromise);
- willingness, eagerness to accept responsibility (necessary to building influence by breaking down the walls and entering the mainstream of school life);
- task competence (especially, knowledge of library administration to deal with issues quickly and expeditiously, as well as knowledge of collaboration, instruction, and exploitation of resources to add value to planning);
- understanding of colleagues and their needs (more easily and credibly done with classroom experience but also without presumption; ask nonjudgmental and important questions such as "What are *we* looking to accomplish here? Which of these approaches would *you* prefer?");
- skill in dealing with people (the ability to negotiate, to deal with difficult players);
- need to achieve (without a driving force to achieve, to leave a legacy, not much will happen in the face of even limited opposition);
- capacity to motivate (guidance, motivation, influence are necessary to move an agenda forward);
- courage, resolution, steadiness (a plan, an ability to take a step sideways and occasionally backwards, starting with the end in mind);
- capacity to win and hold trust (resources are given to those who are trusted; collaboration is possible only with those whom we trust to understand and to deliver);
- capacity to manage, decide, set priorities (the "urgent" can too often overwhelm the really important; a technician or clerk can manage the facility and collection [whether as well as you is irrelevant], meaning that even if you have no help you need to focus on what makes you unique in the school/district, namely, the role of the professional teacher, and ignore or delegate whatever else you can to whomever you can);

- confidence (the bottom-line characteristic of all leaders is self-confidence; research in teacher-librarianship sometimes refers to this as "tough poise");
- ascendance, dominance, assertiveness (recognizing that assertiveness is a positive trait while aggression may not be);
- adaptability, flexibility of approach (to state the trite: only the flexible will not get bent out of shape!).

Think of a leader whom you admire. Why do you respect her or him? What are her or his characteristics? Can these be learned and developed?

Knowing yourself allows you to challenge your excuses for not being successful. It allows you to analyze the situation more objectively to determine if there is a fit for you. You are then better able to complete the sentences, "My suggestions for my own development are . . . " and "The implications for development of my partnerships may be . . . " This of course takes discipline and time to reflect.

Only you can define your measures of personal success, but leaders do look to make the greatest possible impact over the longest period of time. Know yourself. Have a professional development plan. Continually grow and develop.

CONCLUSION

Leadership is about social influence, enlisting the engagement and support of others in achieving a common task. However, to be influential, one needs to be self-aware, focused, and competent, in order to be able to develop strong relationships and partnerships, in order to exhibit trust, honesty, and respect. One is not merely born with these attributes, but rather they can be developed and learned over time.

Leaders also want to leave a "footprint," a legacy. For teacher-librarians this will be the quality of experiences of teachers and students in the school during one's tenure and the development of student abilities that will form a foundation for future learning.

Teacher-librarians are leaders when they exhibit these traits and move a common agenda forward. They do develop strong and healthy communities of learners, not alone but through their networking and influence. Teacher-librarians also add value as community leaders with a clearly defined niche or area of expertise and contribution. In that sense they are "market-driven" and "customer-focused," understanding deeply the needs, interests, and desires of teachers and administrators and working to connect with them.

These teacher-librarian-leaders are not simply focused on getting their message out but are concerned about connecting agendas, about collaborating, about being "at the table" when instructional issues are identified and analyzed and solutions proposed.

The choice is really yours. What kind of leader do you wish to become? What kind of relationships do you wish to develop? What kind of impact do you intend to have? What kind of difference do you expect to make in the lives of teachers and students?

REFERENCES

Bennis, W. 1989. *Why leaders can't lead: The unconscious conspiracy continues.* San Francisco: Jossey-Bass.

Blanchard, K. 1994. Taking the lead when you're not in charge, *Emergency Librarian* 21 (3): 34.

Brown, J. 1999. Leadership for school improvement. In *Foundations for effective school library media programs*, ed. K. Haycock, 27–40. Libraries Unlimited.

Buckingham, M., and D. Clifton. 2001. *Now, discover your strengths*. New York: Free Press.

Chemers, M. 1997. *An integrative theory of leadership*. Englewood Cliffs, NJ: Lawrence Erlbaum.

Cohen, W. A. 2007. *A class with Drucker: The lost lessons of the world's greatest management teacher*. New York: AMACOM.

Gardner, J. 1990. *On leadership*. New York: Free Press.

Goldstein, N., S. Martin, and R. Cialdini. 2008. *Yes!: 50 scientifically proven ways to be persuasive*. New York: Free Press.

Gorman, M. 1982. A good heart and an organized mind. In *Library leadership: Visualizing the future*, ed. D. R. Riggs, 74. Phoenix, AZ: Oryx Press.

Hamel, G. 2009. 25 stretch goals for management. http://blogs.harvardbusiness.org/hamel/2009/02/25_stretch_goals_for_management.html (accessed April 10, 2009).

Hartzell, G. 2003. *Building influence for the school librarian: Tenets, targets and tactics* (2nd ed.). Worthington, OH: Linworth.

Haycock, K., ed. 1990. *Program advocacy: Power, publicity and the teacher-librarian*. Englewood, CO: Libraries Unlimited.

Hirsh, S., and J. Kummerow. 1998. *Introduction to type in organizations* (3rd ed.). Mountain View, CA: CPP.

Kroeger, O., J. M. Thuesen, and H. Rutledge. 2002. *Type talk at work: How the 16 personality types determine your success on the job* (rev. ed.). Delta.

Lencioni, P. 2002. *The five dysfunctions of a team: A leadership fable*. San Francisco: Jossey-Bass.
———. 2005. *Overcoming the five dysfunctions of a team: A field guide for leaders, managers and facilitators*. San Francisco: Jossey-Bass.

Liesveld, R., and J. Miller. 2005. *Teach with your strengths: How great teachers inspire their students*. New York: Gallup Press.

Martin, A. 2007. *The changing nature of leadership: A CCL Research White Paper*. Greensboro, NC: Center for Creative Leadership. http://www.ccl.org/leadership/pdf/research/NatureLeadership.pdf (accessed May 13, 2009).

Myers, I. 1998. *Introduction to type: A guide to understanding your results on the Myers-Briggs Type Indicator* (6th ed.). Revised by L. Kirby and K. Myers. Mountain View, CA: CPP.

Oberg, D. 1999. The school library program and the culture of the school. In *Foundations for effective school library media programs*, ed. K. Haycock, 41–47. Englewood, CO: Libraries Unlimited.

Patterson, K., et al. 2007. *Influencer: The power to change anything*. New York: McGraw-Hill.

Rath, T., and B. Conchie. 2008. *Strengths-based leadership: Great leaders, teams and why people follow*. New York: Gallup Press.

Weisinger, H. 1997. *Emotional intelligence at work*. San Francisco: Jossey-Bass.

2

Librarians as Learning Leaders: Cultivating Cultures of Inquiry

Violet H. Harada

What is the business of libraries if not to cultivate learning? Having raised this rhetorical question, I hasten to add that the challenge for librarians to assume the mantle of leadership requires serious thinking about what this really means. Let me begin by identifying several core beliefs that I share with respected educators. These beliefs frame my reflections in this chapter:

- Learning is not about raising test scores. It is about building a foundation of responsible, reflective, rigorous, and resilient thinking (Costa 2008; Marzano, Waters, and McNulty 2005).
- Accountability includes the actions of adults, not merely the grades and scores of students. This requires a critical examination of what we offer students and how we offer it as a community of providers (Reeves 2006).
- Leadership is not an isolated or isolating activity. It succeeds only in a culture of team-ness (Fullan 2003; Elmore 2000).

In this chapter, I expand on the following major points with the hope that my comments generate spirited and meaningful dialogue amongst readers:

- Critical dimensions of thoughtful learning
- Qualities and dispositions of learning leaders
- Librarians as potential leaders in learning

CRITICAL DIMENSIONS OF THOUGHTFUL LEARNING

Learning involves building one's own understanding about the world. It is a nonlinear and messy process that requires invention and self-organization on the part of the learner. Reflection is essential for meaning making, and dialogue must be encouraged within a community to engender further thinking (Fosnot and Perry 2005). The following dimensions of learning overlap; at the same time, they provide important perspectives on what is essential for the learning leader to know.

Learning Is *Not Just about Facts*: It Encompasses More Than Cognitive Knowledge

Factual knowledge and skills are certainly critical; however, they are only part of the fuzzy ball defined as learning. Learning is not a fixed world of knowledge that the student must come to know. Instead, it is dynamic, constantly morphing, and filled with both uncertainties and possibilities. The sum total involves the learners' "emotions, bodily sensations, ideas, beliefs, values, character qualities, and inferences [they] generate from interactions with others" (Costa 2008, 23). Jean Donham (2007) makes an important distinction between being a learner and being learned. While the latter will remain a critical component of the curriculum, she maintains that "the development of dispositions toward learning and skills to continue to learn will be of utmost importance in [students'] lifetimes" (9).

In establishing the *Standards for the 21st-Century Learner* (2007), the American Association of School Librarians recognized the complex, holistic nature of what we expect learners to demonstrate. The student as the owner of his or her learning must assume responsibilities and engage in self-reflection. Schools as learning organizations (Fullan 2003) must support a culture of inquiry that ultimately challenges students "to question, struggle with possibilities, and create personal meaning from sharing knowledge and learning with others" (Zmuda and Harada 2008, 86).

Learning *Goes Beyond Comprehension*: It Requires Demonstration of Critical Understanding

In his work with Harvard University's Project Zero, David Perkins (1992) maintains that understanding is not a state of possession but one of enablement. He states that when we understand something, we not only possess certain information about it, but we must also be "enabled to do certain things with that knowledge" (77). Barbara Stripling (2007), long an advocate for deep learning through libraries, views learning for understanding as developing the skills and dispositions to interpret and interact with the world. She stresses that both process and content must be addressed for learners to acquire the conceptual and thematic knowledge embedded in the various disciplines (the *what* of learning) at the same time that they develop abilities to demonstrate this knowledge in different contexts and transfer it to various learning environments (the *how* of learning). These processes include the abilities to connect, observe, analyze, challenge, interpret, and infer. Over time and through practice and reflection, learners develop reasoned approaches to meeting their information needs.

Learning Should Be *Hands On and Minds On*: It Requires Active Intellectual Engagement

Art Costa (2008), who has written extensively on habits of mind, aptly says that learning is "not a spectator sport" (22). He maintains that education should be about "thinking to learn and learning to think" (22). Learners *think to learn* by connecting with relevant and generative questions that provoke more questions and stretch the imagination.

They *learn to think* by labeling and identifying cognitive processes. They begin to question their own and others' assumptions and employ such strategies as thinking maps and visual tools to make their learning explicit and visible (Hyerle 2004). This learning requires a safe, nonjudgmental environment where instructors urge students to seriously think about their own thinking and assess their own performance (Costa 2008).

Learning Demands *Connections*: It Requires Construction of Knowledge That Is Personally Meaningful

Real learning has very little to do with traditional schooling practices that often result in mindless regurgitation and the mechanical completion of term papers. Instead, it has everything to do with the learner's steady building of personal knowledge through concrete experience, collaborative discourse, and self-examination. This notion of learning reflects a constructivist theory that envisions learners obtaining information from their senses and through contact with the larger culture to shape a personal view of the world (Clarke 1990).

Constructivist learning draws on current studies in cognitive psychology, philosophy, and anthropology and is frequently messy and recursive because knowledge construction requires sifting of information, selective combination of elements, and comparison of new information with prior knowledge (Fosnot and Perry 2005; Clarke 1990). Learning from this perspective

involves both the process and result of questioning, interpreting, analyzing information; using this information and thinking process to develop, build, and alter our meaning and understanding of concepts and ideas; and integrating current experiences with our past experiences and what we already know about a given subject. (Marlowe and Page 1998, 10)

Instructors assume a key role in encouraging connections between impersonal, abstract concepts and issues existing in the student's world. They "pose problems of emerging relevance to learners, structure learning around big ideas or primary concepts, seek and value students' points of view, adapt curriculum to address students' suppositions, and assess student learning in the context of teaching" (Brooks and Brooks 1993, viii).

Learning Is about *Thinking Together*: It Involves a Social Process of Making Meaning

Constructive dialogue and problem solving within a community are key to a learner-centered process of concept development and decision making (Fosnot and Perry 2005). Clear and respectful dialogue is essential if our goal is to build

a more thought-filled world where we search for ways to care for one another and learn together ... to value the diversity of other cultures, races, time perspectives, political and economic views, and show greater consciousness of how humans affect Earth's limited resources. (Costa 2008, 24)

Instructors help to nurture these collaborative relationships when they purposefully design opportunities for groups to view issues from multiple perspectives, encourage the critical exchange of newfound knowledge, and provoke deeper and more creative questions that fuel new investigations.

QUALITIES AND DISPOSITIONS OF LEARNING LEADERS

If learning requires the elements described in the above section, what must a leader in learning believe in and demonstrate? There are numerous theories of leadership; however, two in particular that resonate with the notion of leadership in the context of learning are *servant leadership* and *instructional leadership*. Robert Greenleaf (1977) states that this form of leadership emerges from a desire to help others. Such leaders do not have to be at the top of the hierarchy, but they are positioned at the center of the organization, that is, they maintain contact with all aspects of the organization and the individuals within it (Marzano, Waters, and McNulty 2005). The central dynamic is nurturing others within the organization. Critical skills possessed by servant leaders include "understanding the personal needs of people within the organization, being a steward of the resources, developing the skills of colleagues within the organization, and being an effective listener" (Marzano, Waters, and McNulty 2005, 16–17).

Like servant leaders, instructional leaders serve as resource providers and instructional resources, perform as effective communicators, and maintain a visible presence in the educational community (Smith and Andrews 1989). They encourage and promote collaborative efforts among teachers and foster coaching relationships (Blasé and Blasé 1999). As mentors, they employ research-based principles of adult learning. They also believe in action research as a systematic method of inquiry that is problem focused and context specific (Gordon 2007).

The attributes embedded in the servant and instructional leadership models are relevant for leaders in the learning context. Here are some of the critical actions and beliefs of learning leaders who walk the talk and model by example.

Learning Leaders Facilitate the Creation of a Shared Vision and Mission Regarding Student Learning

Leaders must be able to create not just personal visions but shared visions (Bennis 2003). For learning leaders, a mission-centered mindset focuses on student achievement. Such a mindset requires a "collective efficacy and capability to develop and use assets to accomplish goals that matter to all community members through agreed-upon processes" (Marzano, Waters, and McNulty 2005, 99).

It is critical to note that the mere statement of a vision or a mission is inadequate. Improvement begins only when the mission "becomes a disciplined mindset that drives the purpose" for all stakeholders in a school community (Zmuda and Harada 2008, 2). To cultivate this mindset, a leader must work collaboratively with other members of the community to achieve thoughtful consensus on critical questions about learning. These questions include:

- What learning matters to students? What will they find interesting, challenging, and valuable?
- How should learning be designed to encourage the use of cognitive and metacognitive skills to develop reflective abilities?
- How might learning be developed to help students maintain mastery goals, take risks, and view errors as inherent in constructing personal knowledge?

- How might we balance students' choice and control over selection of the subject, the approach to the problem, and the artifacts generated, while at the same time providing enough structure so that novices will not be overwhelmed?
- How might we facilitate collaborative work and ensure productive interaction among students?
- What might be the desired outcomes for students in terms of the process and the product? How might we involve students in effectively assessing for learning?

Learning Leaders Understand and Apply the Learning Theories That Serve as the Foundation for Their Vision

To gain a deep appreciation for the roots of current thinking about learning, leaders must be familiar with the works of the scholars that have shaped twenty-first-century reform efforts. For example, they realize that John Dewey's (1972) works on active learning and transfer have had a profound influence on a holistic approach to how students learn best. They value Jerome Bruner's (1971) landmark treatises on education that stress the notion of children as active problem solvers and the curriculum as a spiral that revisits basic ideas and builds upon them until the student demonstrates mastery of the ideas.

Leaders also apply Jean Piaget's (1995) research on the cognitive development of children in their own work in classrooms and library media centers. They test the validity of his theory that early development involves processes based upon physical actions and that later development progresses into more abstract changes in mental operations. At the same time, leaders build on Piaget's notion of equilibration, that is, that all children try to strike a balance between assimilation (applying previous knowledge) and accommodation (changing behavior to account for new knowledge).

They also carefully study Lev Vygotsky's (1986) perspective on the influence of societal factors on the individual's capabilities, as well as his findings about the role of mentors in guiding young learners to achieve their fullest potential. They are familiar with Vygotsky's work on cognitive development as subject to the dialogic interplay between nature and history, biology and culture, and the individual and society (McGregor 2007). They test his concept of the "zone of proximal development," which places instruction at the heart of development, enabling a child's potential for learning when working with more knowledgeable others.

Major learning theories that are central to student learning have emerged from the work of educators and scholars such as the luminaries cited above. I briefly discuss two related theories here. The first is *constructivism*, which has been influenced by the works of Dewey, Piaget, and Bruner. I introduced constructivism earlier in this chapter and return to it here. Constructivism is not a cookbook of how-to strategies but a way of thinking about learning. It places value on the accommodation of existing thinking and the assimilation of aspects of the new experience. The development of thinking involves steps that build successive experiences with the world and that connect ideas with a real-life community. Teaching is a process of facilitation, of guiding participation with more experienced partners, and of designing for learning through contextualized and interactive participation (Kuhlthau, Maniotes, and Caspari 2007).

The second theory is *social constructivism*. While it is related to constructivism, this theory focuses on thinking and learning through social interactions that inform personal constructions of meaning. Influenced by Vygotsky, social constructivism underscores the importance of language not only in eliciting ideas but also in shaping them.

For students, guided participation with more experienced others and the gradual reduction of the instructor's presence would be of highest priority.

Learning Leaders Must Know the Research Underpinning Meaningful Learning

Ross Todd (2007) states, "Research informing practice, and practice informing research is a fundamental cycle in any sustainable profession" (64). Learning leaders must invest the time to carefully examine what research says about how real learning occurs. They share their findings with colleagues to help make informed decisions about teaching and curriculum and to provide them with opportunities to "know the research" (Todd 2007, 64). Here are some examples of the research spanning four decades:

- Active learning methods are superior to teacher-dominated approaches in measures of academic, affective, and skill learning (Slavin 1989; Sharan and Sharan 1989/1990; Darling-Hammond 1993; Secules and Cottom 1997).
- Teacher expectations are key in raising the quality of student achievement (Rosenthal and Jacobson 1968).
- Consistent and regular forms of assessment must be used to inform immediate and decisive interventions (Reeves 2006).

Studies that have dealt specifically with the incorporation of thinking in the curriculum have generally reported that thinking skills accelerated the learning gains of participants (McGregor 2007). Investigations of an experimental or quasi-experimental nature revealed that students who developed these skills outperformed those in control groups.

Scholars in education have also conducted meta-analyses of research to formulate generalizations about the impact of critical thinking in the curriculum. Cotton (1991), for example, summarized findings from 56 research studies and reviews, largely in the United States, that examined the incorporation of higher-order thinking skills in a range of subjects. She indicated that in almost all of these studies, students improved their performances on SAT and other tests as well as in general classroom assignments. These higher-order thinking skills included analysis, synthesis, evaluation, predicting, making inferences, formulating hypotheses, drawing conclusions, elaborating, identifying assumptions, determining bias, and recognizing logical inconsistencies.

Current scholars are raising fundamental questions about the nature of knowledge and whose knowledge counts (e.g., Gadsden 2008; Sperling and DiPardo 2008; Larsen-Freeman and Freeman 2008; Nasir, Hand, and Taylor 2008; Duschl 2008). They are challenging long-standing assumptions about domains of knowledge being fixed and known. Whether in the arts or sciences, in history or languages, international educators state that learning disciplinary knowledge entails more than acquiring basic skills or bits of received knowledge. They agree that the boundaries and practices of academic disciplines are fluid and negotiated (Kelly, Luke, and Green 2008). Their findings have profound implications for what is being taught and how it is being taught in today's school systems.

How do learning leaders keep abreast of this research and literature? They begin by knowing the research in their specializations. For school librarians, it means reading, reflecting, and acting on statewide studies and compilations of research on literacy learning. Scholastic, for example, provides updated versions of capsulated research in *School Libraries Work!* Refereed journals such as *School Library Media Research* and *School Libraries Worldwide* provide access to scholarly articles that allow leaders to develop "an empirical basis for making and justifying decisions, and for identifying gaps on which continuous improvement programs can be built" (Todd 2007, 66). It is also critical to know about the research being conducted in the larger educational arena. Effective starting points would be the publications and conferences sponsored by such organizations as the American Educational Research Association and the Association for Supervision and Curriculum Development. Bringing this research to the attention of colleagues in the school community is a crucial responsibility of the learning leader.

Learning Leaders Engage Students and Peers in Thoughtful Inquiry

Leaders seek to support learning, not control it. They further inquiry, not orthodoxy. June Gould (2005) states:

They continuously evaluate themselves, their students, and the system in which they teach. They collaborate with their students and encourage them to collaborate, not to compete, with one another. They become planners, models, guides, observers of development and facilitators and challengers to children's existing personal models of the world. (108)

Learning for such leaders is not about finding instant answers and easy solutions. It is not about covering the curriculum between the covers of a textbook. Instead, learning leaders invite students and professional colleagues to "experience the world's richness, empower them to ask their own questions and seek their own answers, and challenge them to understand the world's complexities" (Brooks and Brooks 1993, 5). They encourage deeper investigations when the presence of new information prompts people to rethink their prior ideas.

Learning Leaders Believe in the Synergy and Power of Learning Communities and Teamwork

Current paradigms of leadership have shifted from leaders as single individuals to leadership being shared by teams of individuals (Fullan 2003; Elmore 2000; Spillane 2006). Creating and sustaining teams requires that educators view leadership as a distributed, interactive web of leaders and followers who periodically change roles as the situation warrants. Learning leaders must use processes that "enhance communication among members, provide for efficient reconciliation of disagreements, and keep members attuned to the current status of the community" (Marzano, Waters, and McNulty 2005, 100).

The concept of a *learning community* overarches this notion of distributed leadership. Such a community believes in similar goals and shares mutual interests. Members collaborate over time to exchange ideas and find solutions (Lave and Wenger 1991). What holds them together is a common vision, a sense of purpose, and a real need to know what each other knows. In pursuit of these goals and interests, they employ a common set of practices, work with the same tools, and express themselves in a common language. They use one another as sounding boards and teach and learn from each other. In short, they are partners committed to jointly improving practice.

Through the above-mentioned activities, they move progressively toward similar beliefs and value systems that include the following agreements:

- Focusing on *significance*: teams address questions that truly matter and lead to deep, positive impact on learning and practice.
- Demanding *quality*: they hold everyone accountable for processes and student learning results.
- Fostering *integrity*: they cultivate an environment of trust, openness, and respect.
- Practicing *ethics*: they demonstrate fair, just, and compassionate understanding in their actions (Marzano, Waters, and McNulty 2005, 105).

The Bottom Line: Learning Leaders Model the Behaviors and Attitudes They Wish to Inspire in Others

Rather than assuming the stance of the expert delivering most of the content, leaders invite their professional colleagues to "uncover, discover, and reflect on content . . . through inquiry, investigation, research, and analysis in the context of a problem, critical question, issue, or theme" (Marlowe and Page 1998, 11). They design learning for meaningful transfer and application by providing clear information with descriptions and examples of the goals and the performances expected. They allow for practice where learners engage actively and reflectively. They supply informative feedback through clear and thorough counsel. By so doing, leaders help others to discriminate between the relevant and the irrelevant and to look at issues from different perspectives (Marlowe and Page 1998).

Richard Elmore (2000) and Douglas Reeves (2006) elaborate on the following behaviors and attitudes that define leaders as inquirers:

- Being *analytical*: they challenge the status quo with terminology that is clear and vivid.
- Being *relational*: they build trusting and empathetic relationships.
- Being *reflective*: they think critically about lessons learned, record small wins and setbacks, and document conflicts between values and practice.

In short, these leaders model the excitement and rigor of inquiry in their work with the other members of the learning community. They are persistent seekers who ask the hard questions: What did we actually learn today? Whom did we nurture? What difficult issue did we confront? What progress did we make? Where do we go from here?

LIBRARIANS AS POTENTIAL LEADERS IN LEARNING

Might school librarians be potential leaders in learning? They are certainly in positions of opportunity! As many library educators have noted, school librarians work with the entire school community. They may not be experts in every single curriculum area, but they are uniquely situated to gain a critical overview of the entire curricular landscape. However, to be acknowledged as big picture experts, librarians must also have knowledge of current educational trends, emerging technologies, new resources in diverse formats, and community connections (Hughes-Hassell and Harada 2007). In addition, they must be able to identify both teacher and student needs. The following examples are snapshots of librarians functioning as learning leaders. The names and schools are fictitious; however, each example is a composite inspired by actual practices.

Snapshot 1: Librarian as a Model Teacher of Thinking Strategies

Carla has been the librarian at Ocean View Elementary for five years. Over this time, she has steadily built her relationships with the teachers at the school. At this point, more than half of the grade level teachers are working with her on a research-related project each year. She nurtures these relationships by attending grade level curriculum meetings when possible, examining curriculum maps that the teachers are producing, and attending staff development sessions with them. At the same time, she maintains an RSS feed that helps her keep in touch with relevant research and learning-related news on the Web. By engaging in these types of activities, Carla realizes that substantive learning requires teaching for "conceptual coherence" (Stripling 2007, 41). She wants students to understand how and why events happen and what motivates decisions. She also encourages students to appreciate that issues are never black or white, as well as that understanding conflicts from multiple perspectives affords a fuller understanding of how things come to be.

In her teaching, Carla models a range of thinking strategies that help students move toward deeper as well as broader understandings. Her repertoire includes the following strategies that she has culled from the literature (e.g., Tomlinson 2008; Ritchart and Perkins 2008; Taggart 2005):

- When she and a teacher introduce a new unit, Carla provokes curiosity by using a technique called *see-think-wonder*. Using artifacts, demonstrations, and media to stimulate engagement, they challenge the students with the following types of questions: What do you see? What do you think about that? What does it make you wonder?
- They create *word walls* in the library and classroom where students contribute vocabulary that help them grapple with concepts and ideas in different disciplines.
- They design a range of *graphic organizers* for different learning purposes, among them, *fishbone maps* to show causal connections, *T charts* to distinguish pros and cons of issues, *mind maps* to visually connect ideas and supporting details, and *grids* to compare multiple sets of data.
- They engage the students in *role playing* to demonstrate their understanding of different perspectives on issues and problems.
- They encourage students to create *dialogue journals* that help them assess for learning. They recognize the importance of cultivating student voice and the value of responding to students with appropriate and timely feedback. The students ask themselves: What was exciting? What was difficult? What might be the best next step? Why? How might the teacher and librarian help me?
- Importantly, they model a *think-aloud technique* that makes students realize that adults do not come up with instant answers—they fumble, experiment, and learn from failures.

What Carla has discovered is that if she is willing to take the lead in experimenting with the techniques mentioned above—and teachers observe her interaction with the students—they begin to see new instructional possibilities. Carla explains,

The library is like a fishbowl. When I teach, I let the teachers know that I welcome their constructive advice about what I might do better with their students. The teachers really start watching what I am doing when they realize that I sincerely want their feedback. Many of them provide terrific input, which I thank them for and use. But what is really rewarding is that they also learn about additional ways to develop thinking. They tell me, "I never used that approach or technique before but I really like what I saw you doing. I want to try it in my classroom." These types of exchanges help all of us to grow!

Snapshot 2: Librarian as an Active Researcher

Darlene has been a librarian at Pacific Rim Middle School for 10 years. The curriculum focuses on an integrated core of subjects, that is, language arts, science, social studies, and mathematics. Teachers in these disciplines plan as teams and work with students in large, flexible blocks of time. They focus on "blended curriculum topics" and welcome Darlene's involvement in the students' projects. Darlene, in turn, seizes this opportunity to be part of the teams. She discovers that while the teachers are enthused about students "conducting research," they have limited understanding about research as a process. They are unaware that students need guided support in key phases of their research projects. One team works especially well together and appears open to suggestions that improve the learning and teaching environment. Darlene feels very comfortable with the members of this team and she proposes that they think about the following big questions that drive their work: What do we want students to be able to accomplish in their research projects? What help will they need to demonstrate achievement of these goals? How can we tell if students have succeeded? She volunteers to serve as the coordinator for this work and the teachers are willing to participate if she takes the lead.

What Darlene is attempting is an exciting dimension of leadership that requires not only knowledge of existing research but engagement in research that connects directly with practice. *Action research* is a "systematic approach to problem-solving and understanding phenomena in depth that can be woven into the fabric of everyday work patterns and routines" (Gordon 2007, 162). The research questions are relevant because the findings are immediately applicable to the workplace. Action research employs the same methodologies as formal qualitative research and "must meet the same standards of validity and reliability, although findings are not usually generalizable from sample to population because sample sizes are generally small" (Gordon 2007, 163). This form of research is sometimes referred to as *reflection-on-action* and *reflection-in-action* (McGregor 2007).

As the facilitator, Darlene works with the team to refine their research questions. By reading and discussing various works, including Kuhlthau's investigations on the information search process (2004), they gain considerable insight into the complex nature of the process. They also brainstorm possible techniques and intervention strategies they might incorporate at different phases of the research process. Importantly, they discuss the criteria to assess learner outcomes and the instruments they might use to conduct the assessments. Darlene works with the team to draft a tentative timeline for the action research that synchronizes with the work of the students. While Darlene maintains overall responsibilities for keeping things moving, the teaching and assessment are divided amongst the team. She creates a wiki workspace where the team members jointly edit specific lesson plans connected with the unit, work on drafts of the assessment tools, and collect and comment on assessment results.

The team discovers that the most effective interventions are focused on the following: (1) more time spent on the "presearch" phase for students to acquire sufficient background knowledge; (2) direct teaching to help students distinguish relevant from irrelevant details, detect bias in information, and evaluate Web sources; and (3) involvement of students in self-assessment at checkpoints throughout the process. The critical insight for teachers on the team is the notion of *research as a process*. In her culminating log, one of the teachers reflects,

I have to admit that before we collaborated on this unit with Darlene, I always skimmed through stuff at the beginning. I didn't really think about the importance of the presearch phase. Actually, I didn't KNOW about the presearch phase. I never really thought too much about the fact that the students might not understand the assignment. I never considered that they didn't have a big picture about the general topic. I never gave them time to examine the quality of their questions. I just assumed that they could get the information they needed without spending any time teaching them how to do this well. I guess what I am saying is that I never really saw this whole thing as a PROCESS for my students.

A second teacher acknowledges,

I came to understand the power of action research. It isn't something done in an ivory tower. It is practical and real. We observe what students are doing, involve them in assessment, study the results, and improve things as we work. I know we wouldn't have done this without Darlene. She was the catalyst and the cheerleader. She kept asking the hard questions, like: What is the data telling us? How do we make this better? What would happen if? Are there other approaches? What else might we do?

Snapshot 3: Librarian as a Builder of Professional Learning Communities

Sam and Marilyn are co-librarians at Paradise Valley High School, where faculty and administration are experimenting with the formation of professional learning communities. Sam joined the staff 12 years ago and Marilyn 2 years ago. They share common beliefs about improving student performance through project-based learning. They proactively seek opportunities to collaborate with teachers and maintain a visible presence on the campus (e.g., Sam is on the school's vision team and Marilyn serves on the technology committee).

At Paradise Valley, faculty members recognize that most of the staff development in previous years has been haphazard and ineffectual. As one of the administrators wryly observes, "We tend to jump on the latest bandwagon and the wagons change every year." At the beginning of the school year, teachers determine the major issues to be studied within the different professional learning communities. Faculty members select the community they wish to join. One of the communities deals with collaborative problem solving for students. Sam and Marilyn volunteer to jointly facilitate this particular community because they have been addressing the same topic with feeder school librarians in their neighborhood (i.e., elementary and middle schools that "feed" into Paradise Valley). The essential question for this community is: How can we foster productive and responsible interaction among students?

As co-facilitators for this particular community, Marilyn and Sam stimulate inquiry and reflection on the research relevant to group learning processes. To cultivate respect and trust amongst colleagues, they target the following goals:

• Mutually agree on outcomes that are clearly focused on what matters to the community.
• Allow for all members to contribute their ideas; encourage diverse and contrary opinions.

- Collectively consider possible strategies and actions to promote effective group work and carefully analyze the strengths and weaknesses in the process.
- While implementing strategies and actions, provide opportunities to assess whether the strategies are working as expected and whether modifications might be necessary.
- Establish clear and supportive lines of communication.
- Invite reflections and evaluations from all participants. Some of the questions they ask are: Are the strategies being employed successfully? Would a different approach be more effective? What conclusions can we reach?

The two librarians concur that leading a learning community stretches them as professionals. Marilyn states:

We are finding out how isolated most of us are in a school. We close our doors and we don't know what others are doing. In this professional community, we open the doors and this can be intimidating for many people. Sam and I are discovering how important it is to make everyone feel comfortable and trustful. We learn how it's critical to focus on the students, not ourselves. We move away from what we have traditionally done to what actually works! It's an eye-opening experience for all of us.

Sam adds:

Marilyn and I have to be cheerleaders, coordinators, and catalysts. We really prepare hard for the meetings because we want quality time spent on clearly focused goals for each session. We also have to be sensitive to what's going on in the school and use this information to address current and potential problems. This has been intense work but it has also been exhilarating!

Snapshot 4: Librarian as an Advocate for Evidence-Based Practice of Student Learning

Lorraine and Paige are librarians at two different schools in the state. They have 7 and 15 years of experience in their respective schools. Their common bond is that they are officers of the state's school library organization. In their leadership capacity, Lorraine and Paige have been studying state reports on student achievement. With increasing alarm, they realize that nowhere in these reports is there mention of the library's role in student learning. They form a small study group of librarians to determine how best to approach this problem. They conclude that libraries must engage in evidence-based practice—what Todd (2003) describes as the "day-to-day professional work that is directed toward demonstrating the tangible impact and outcomes of sound decision making and implementation of organizational goals and objectives" (7).

After several sessions brainstorming ways to approach this task, the group decides to develop *evidence folders* (Harada 2006; Harada and Yoshina 2005). They approach this task in the following manner:

- *Determine school goals and priorities.* They recognize that the administration will invest most of the school's human and financial resources to meet the targeted school priorities. Identifying these goals, then, is a critical first step in strategic planning.
- *Determine the library's contribution to the goals.* By carefully identifying the major direction of the school program, they also decide where to channel their time and resources. By doing this, they emphasize the value-added nature of what they have to offer.

- *Identify specific learning targets.* They teach a wide spectrum of skills in their respective programs. Because they work with entire school populations, it would be impossible for them to formally assess every lesson taught. They recognize the need to be selective. Questions that help them make workable decisions include: Which learning targets are most directly related to the school's goals? How do the library's targets match the classroom's learning goals? Which classes or grade levels might be most willing to collaborate with the library?
- *Establish criteria to measure student achievement of the learning targets.* They realize that in assessment-focused instruction, instructors must start with an idea of what the students should demonstrate at the end of the learning experience. Grant Wiggins and Jay McTighe (1998) have popularized the term "backward design" (146) to describe this important concept in curriculum planning. The criteria should be stated so that they are understandable not only to the instructors but also to the students.
- *Devise assessment tools.* They use a range of techniques and instruments including rubrics, rating scales, checklists, and logs. Whichever tool is used, the criteria must be clearly stated so that both students and instructional teams can apply them to determine levels of achievement.
- *Collect and analyze the data.* By systematically collecting the data and figuring ways to summarize and analyze the information, they use the results to drive improvements in learning and teaching. The group finds that a useful technique is to enter the data on a spreadsheet. This allows them multiple options for formatting, sorting, calculating, and presenting the results.
- *Communicate the results to different stakeholder groups.* The same assessment data can be packaged and presented in formats appropriate for different stakeholder groups, including students, teachers, parents, and administrators. With students and parents, the critical focus is the individual student's progress and accomplishments. Instructional partners need the same student-by-student accounting; at the same time, they also require class profiles of this information. Administrators, however, desire broader summaries where the data might be aggregated by grade levels or by courses.

Lorraine and Paige also decide to move to another level of leadership by designing a course on evidence-based practice for school librarians. They collaborate with the university and the state department of education to design the course as a tri-organization initiative. The course is offered as a three-day summer institute with follow-up work in the ensuing school year. This extension into the school year is conducted online and through videoconferences.

CONCLUSION

Learning leaders recognize that schools are places of growth for adults as well as children. As leaders, they have a commitment to continual improvement for everyone. This means that thinking about learning is not enough. It must be acted upon.

In schools that are learning organizations (Fullan 2003), all participants become aware of critical and generative thinking and how such thinking is cultivated. They believe in the fulfilling capacity of inquiry for others and for themselves. They recognize that conflict, uncertainty, and diversity are inherent in the learning and change processes (Kaser et al. 2006).

Can school librarians step forward as such leaders? Do they have the vision and the drive to challenge the status quo? Do they embrace the moral imperative to assist all students in developing and refining their personal models of the world? Can they be the go-to persons for research-based evidence? Can they ask tough and thoughtful questions about how research interfaces with daily practice? Do they possess the resilience and tenacity to deal with dissent and resistance and to move groups toward positive action?

I believe that librarians are not only ready but that librarians are vital lifelines to learning. From countless conversations and visits with educators across the nation, I have come away with inspiring accounts of librarians as negotiators, enablers, and catalysts, who acknowledge problems and work toward solutions that strengthen attitudes, knowledge, and skills in the teaching-learning environment. Allison Zmuda and I concluded in *Librarians as Learning Specialists* (2008) that the power of the librarian to contribute to the school has "never been more vital, more feasible, or more exciting than it is today" (117). If learning is a long and fascinating adventure, librarians are ready to blaze the trails!

REFERENCES

American Association of School Librarians. 2007. *Standards for the 21st-century learner*. http://www.ala.org/ala/mgrps/divs/aasl/guidelinesandstandards/learningstandards/standards.cfm (accessed March 29, 2009).

Bennis, Warren. 2003. *On becoming a leader*. New York: Basic Books.

Blasé, Joseph, and Jo Blasé. 1999. Principals' instructional leadership and teacher development: Teachers' perspectives. *Educational Administration Quarterly* 35 (3): 349–380.

Brooks, Jacqueline Grennon, and Martin G. Brooks. 1993. *In search of understanding: The case for constructivist classrooms*. Alexandria, VA: Association for Supervision and Curriculum Development.

Bruner, Jerome. 1971. *The relevance of education*. New York: W.W. Norton and Co.

Clarke, John H. 1990. *Patterns of thinking: Integrating learning skills in content teaching*. Boston: Allyn and Bacon.

Costa, Arthur L. 2008. The thought-filled curriculum. *Educational Leadership* 65 (5): 20–24.

Cotton, Kathleen. 1991. *Teaching thinking skills*. School Improvement Research Series (SIRS). Portland, OR: Northwest Regional Education Laboratory. http://www.nwrel.org/scpd/sirs/6/cu11.html (accessed March 29, 2009).

Darling-Hammond, L. 1993. Reframing the school reform agenda: Developing capacity for school transformation." *Phi Delta Kappan* 74 (10): 752–761.

Dewey, John. 1972. *Experience and education*. New York: Collier Books. (Original work published in 1938).

Donham, Jean. 2007. Graduating students who are not only learned but also learners. *Teacher Librarian* 35 (1): 8–12.

Duschl, Richard. 2008. Science education in three-part harmony: Balancing conceptual, epistemic, and social learning goals. *Review of Research in Education* 32: 268–291.

Elmore, Richard. 2000. *Building a new structure for school leadership*. Washington, DC: Albert Shanker Institute.

Fosnot, Catherine Twomey, and Randall Steward Perry. 2005. Constructivism: A psychological theory of learning. In *Constructivism: Theory, perspectives, and practice* (2nd ed.), ed. Catherine Twomey Fosnot, 8–38. New York: Teachers College.

Fullan, Michael. 2003. *Change forces: With a vengeance*. London: RoutledgeFalmer.

Gadsden, Vivian L. 2008. The arts and education: Knowledge generation, pedagogy, and the discourse of learning. *Review of Research in Education* 32: 29–61.

Gordon, Carol A. 2007. The real thing: Authentic teaching through action research. In *School reform and the school library media specialist*, eds. Sandra Hughes-Hassell and Violet H. Harada, 161–178. Westport, CT: Libraries Unlimited.

Gould, June S. 2005. A constructivist perspective on teaching and learning in the language arts. In *Constructivism: Theory, perspectives, and practice* (2nd ed.), ed. Catherine Twomey Fosnot, 99–109. New York: Teachers College.

Greenleaf, Robert. 1977. *Servant leadership: A journey into the nature of legitimate power and greatness.* New York: Paulist Press.

Harada, Violet H. 2006. Building evidence folders for learning through library media centers. *School Library Media Activities Monthly,* 23 (3): 25–30.

Harada, Violet H., and Joan M. Yoshina. 2005. *Assessing learning: Librarians and teachers as partners.* Westport, CT: Libraries Unlimited.

Hughes-Hassell, Sandra, and Violet H. Harada. 2007. Change agentry: An essential role for library media specialists. In *School reform and the school library media specialist,* eds. Sandra Hughes-Hassell and Violet H. Harada, 1–15. Westport, CT: Libraries Unlimited.

Hyerle, David, ed. 2004. *Student successes with thinking maps: School-based research, results, and models for achievement using visual tools.* Thousand Oaks, CA: Corwin Press.

Kaser, Joyce, Susan Mundry, Katherine E. Stiles, and Susan Loucks-Horsley. 2006. *Leading every day: 124 actions for effective leadership* (2nd ed.). Thousand Oaks, CA: Corwin Press.

Kelly, Gregory J., Allan Luke, and Judith Green. 2008. Introduction: What counts as knowledge in educational settings: Disciplinary knowledge, assessment, and curriculum. *Review of Research in Education* 32: vii–x.

Kuhlthau, Carol Collier. 2004. *Seeking meaning: A process approach to library and information services* (2nd ed.). Westport, CT: Libraries Unlimited.

Kuhlthau, Carol Collier, Leslie K. Maniotes, and Ann K. Caspari. 2007. *Guided inquiry: Learning in the 21st century.* Westport, CT: Libraries Unlimited.

Larsen-Freeman, Diane, and Donald Freeman. 2008. Language moves: The place of "foreign" languages in classroom teaching and learning. *Review of Research in Education* 32: 147–186.

Lave, Jean, and Etienne Wenger. 1991. *Situated learning: Legitimate peripheral participation.* Cambridge, UK: Cambridge University Press.

Marlowe, Bruce A., and Marilyn L. Page. 1998. *Creating and sustaining the constructivist classroom.* Thousand Oaks, CA: Corwin Press.

Marzano, Robert J., Timothy Waters, and Brian A. McNulty. 2005. *School leadership that works: From research to results.* Alexandria, VA: Association for Supervision and Curriculum Development.

McGregor, Debra. 2007. *Developing thinking, developing learning: A guide to thinking skills in education.* Berkshire, UK: Open University Press.

Nasir, Na'ilah Suad, Victoria Hand, and Edd V. Taylor. 2008. Culture and mathematics in school: Boundaries between "cultural" and "domain" knowledge in the mathematics classroom and beyond. *Review of Research in Education* (32): 187–240.

Perkins, David. 1992. *Smart schools: From training memories to educating minds.* New York: Free Press.

Piaget, Jean. 1995. Essay on the theory of qualitative values in static sociology. In *Sociological Studies,* ed. Jean Piaget, 97–133. New York: Routledge. (Original work published in 1941.)

Reeves, Douglas B. 2006. *The learning leader: How to focus school improvement for better results.* Alexandria, VA: Association for Supervision and Curriculum Development.

Ritchart, Ron, and David Perkins. 2008. Making thinking visible. *Educational Leadership* 65 (5): 57–61.

Rosenthal, Robert, and Lenore Jacobson. 1968. *Pygmalion in the classroom: Teacher expectation and pupils' intellectual development.* New York: Holt, Rinehart and Winston.

Secules, Teresa, and Carolyn Cottom. 1997. Creating schools for thought. *Educational Leadership* 54 (6): 56–59.

Sharan, Yael, and Shlomo Sharan. 1989/1990. Group investigation expands cooperative learning. *Educational Leadership* 47 (4):17–21.

Slavin, Robert E. 1989. Cooperative learning and student achievement. In *School and classroom organization,* ed. Robert E. Slavin, 129–158. Englewood Cliffs, NJ: Lawrence Erlbaum.

Smith, Wilma F., and Richard L. Andrews. 1989. *Instructional leadership: How principals make a difference.* Alexandria, VA: Association for Supervision and Curriculum Development.

Sperling, Melanie, and Anne DiPardo. 2008. English education research and classroom practice: New directions for new times. *Review of Research in Education* (32): 62–108.

Spillane, James P. 2006. *Distributed leadership.* San Francisco, CA: Jossey-Bass.

Stripling, Barbara K. 2007. Teaching for understanding. In *School reform and the school library media specialist,* eds. Sandra Hughes-Hassell and Violet H. Harada, 37–55. Westport, CT: Libraries Unlimited.

Taggart, Germaine. 2005. *Promoting reflective thinking in teachers: 50 action strategies.* Thousand Oaks, CA: Corwin Press.

Todd, Ross J. 2003. Evidence-based practice: Overview, rationale, and challenges. In *We boost achievement! Evidence-based practice for school library media specialists,* ed. David V. Loertscher, 1–25. Salt Lake City, UT: Hi Willow Research and Publishing.

———. 2007. Evidence-based practice and school libraries: From advocacy to action. In *School reform and the school library media specialist,* eds. Sandra Hughes-Hassell and Violet H. Harada, 57–78. Westport, CT: Libraries Unlimited.

Tomlinson, Carol Ann. 2008. The goals of differentiation. *Educational Leadership* 65 (3): 26–30.

Vygotsky, Lev. 1986. *Thought and language* (rev. ed.). Cambridge, MA: MIT Press.

Wiggins, Grant, and Jay McTighe. 1998. *Understanding by design.* Alexandria, VA: Association for Supervision and Curriculum Development.

Zmuda, Allison, and Violet H. Harada. 2008. *Librarians as learning specialists: Meeting the learning imperative for the 21st century.* Westport, CT: Libraries Unlimited.

3

The School Librarian
as an Advocacy Leader

Deb Levitov

WHAT IS ADVOCACY?

> Leadership and advocacy often resemble a dance more than a straight-line march toward a goal.... At times the leader advocate must work the process and lead the dance; at other times, the leader must stand back and let the process work, always ready to add a step or two to the dance when necessary. (Stripling 2007, 54)

According to the American Association of School Librarians (AASL), advocacy is

an on-going process of building partnerships so that others will act for and with you, turning passive support into educated action for the library media program. It begins with a vision and a plan for the library media program that is then matched to the agenda and priorities of stakeholders. ("Advocacy")

This is a definition that school librarians must understand and internalize before developing an advocacy plan. It goes beyond public relations and marketing and gets to the heart of what it takes to be a leader in garnering support and leverage for school libraries.

VARIATIONS OF ADVOCACY

There are two levels of advocacy: (1) personal advocacy—one-on-one advocacy that comes from the school librarian, and (2) group advocacy—organized efforts at the state and national levels by school librarians and/or others. The latter can involve stakeholder advocacy—involving those who have an investment in school library programs (e.g., students, teachers, administrators, frontline workers, parents, other community members) and who speak out on behalf of school libraries. This becomes the most powerful advocacy of all—when others speak up for and about school library programs and school librarians. It erases any question that the effort is self-serving, with school librarians defending their jobs or whining about their circumstances. It instead reflects the presence of a shared mission for the school library.

As Ken Haycock has so aptly stated, "it is not about us" (2004, 6). People do things for their own reasons, and school librarians must find out what those reasons are and make the connections in order to build strong advocacy efforts. Through this type of communication, others will be drawn into not only understanding but defining the purpose of the school library, how it contributes to student learning, and how the school librarian can be a partner in teaching. In this way, through their own firsthand experiences, stakeholders become advocates who speak up for and about school libraries and the role of the school librarian, acting for and with them.

Often public relations and marketing efforts are thought to equal advocacy. Although public relations and marketing are key to moving advocacy plans forward, true advocacy is deeper, more meaningful, and more effective than public relations or marketing alone. The purpose of this chapter is to provide examples of advocacy led by school librarians at all levels. The examples given will help school librarians conceptualize their leadership role and also understand how to personalize multifaceted advocacy plans that are ongoing and effective in their settings.

EFFECTIVE ADVOCACY

To be effective advocates, school librarians must be leaders, professional learners, teachers, visionaries, and connectors (Levitov 2007, 30). Advocacy is something that the school librarian must do every day, all year long. But it is an effort that must go beyond the school librarian as the sole voice advocating for the program; it must be an effort to get others to speak for and about the school library. School librarians must show how the school library program connects to and advances the goals of the would-be advocates (such as teachers, administrators, school board members, legislators, and so on), by fitting within their context, speaking their language, and linking to their agenda. Advocacy is a process of helping stakeholders build personalized perceptions of school libraries and become spokespersons for the mission they help define. It is a process that requires leadership skills on the part of the school librarian.

In a literature review by Shannon, research by Burks, 1993; Farwell, 1998; Hughes, 1998; and Johnson, 1993 showed that "school library media specialists' confidence, initiative, communication skills and leadership qualities were important factors for those who were active players in the total school curriculum and instructional program" (Shannon 2002). In summary, there is

overwhelming evidence of the importance for school library media specialists to possess effective communication and interpersonal skills. These competencies appear basic to all aspects of the work of school library media specialists and are judged essential by school administrators, teachers and school library media specialists themselves. (Shannon, 2002)

These leadership skills are a prerequisite for all forms of advocacy.

To advance the efforts of advocacy, school librarians need a vision for moving the school library program forward into the center of the learning community. This vision must align with the needs of the twenty-first-century learner and the role of the twenty-first-century educator. It must provide an image that transforms the library stereotypes held by stakeholders. This must be a vision for recreating the school library into an entity that champions learning and inquiry. According to David Loertscher, this school library is a unique environment . . . a learning commons. At the November 2009 Treasure Mountain Research Forum, Ross Todd described this learning commons

as an entity that removes barriers, provides a safe haven for using diverse and conflicting sources, while providing access to quality and rich information—all of which leads to deep learning. This new school library facilitates networked learning, enables inquiry, the building of knowledge, and provides for inspiration and creativity. (Levitov 2009)

This is the image that must be recreated with stakeholders, so that they too can see the role of the school library in planning for education in the twenty-first century.

In addition to developing a vision for the school library, school librarians need a plan of action and a keen sense of connecting the school library program with what is important to others (Levitov 2007). This plan for connecting the school library program to the agendas of others demonstrates an understanding of curriculum, the academic goals of the school, and the local, state, and national trends in education; articulates the central role of technology and resource sharing in education; and outlines how the school library can be involved in and facilitate the efforts. To be a leader of advocacy, the school librarian must involve others in building a vision and designing a plan that will recreate the school library. In this way, the stakeholders come to understand the mission outlined for the school library and are vested in moving the plan forward and creating the program imagined.

Being proactive is essential to this task and requires making connections, serving on committees, being present when decisions are made, and making significant contributions (Levitov 2007). Leaders have to take risks. As Sara Kelly Johns, former AASL president stated, "Visibility in our state and national professional organization as well as in our community is an essential part of our job" (2007). Johns emphasizes that school librarians "need others to tell our library story, to advocate on our behalf. Parents and students are absolutely the best advocates. . . . But, you need to be vocal too. If you aren't, a piece of the puzzle is missing" (2007). As an effective advocate, the school librarian can, in turn, grow advocates.

ADVOCACY WITH ADMINISTRATORS

Administrators are identified as key players in the success of the school library program and the success of the school librarian (Campbell 1994; Oberg, Hay, and Henri 2000; Rose 2002). As reflected in the professional literature, administrators receive little formal training about school libraries in their administrative coursework (Levitov 2009). Nor are administrators familiar with the roles a school librarian can play in the school academic program (O'Neal 2004; Levitov 2009).

Lack of Knowledge

The well-planned, -supported, -developed, and -used school library program has immense potential. It can offer limitless possibilities. Yet a large percentage of administrators lack the background knowledge needed to conceptualize and build strong programs. They are put in charge of a center containing thousands of resources and a multitude of equipment worth thousands of dollars, and they know virtually nothing about it—other than what they bring from personal experience, from brief coverage in their coursework about copyright, or from budgeting that touches on library acquisitions.

Many school administrators rely on the school librarian in their building or district to inform them about the school library program. They enter their professional careers viewing the school librarian in traditional library roles. Yet, they do not always have a vision for the school library as a learning center and often have a limited sense of the value or possibilities that lie within. In a study involving 13 administrators from across the country, most were unaware of the standards developed for school libraries, research available about them, resources available to manage and guide them, or the roles outlined for school librarians in national guidelines (Levitov 2009).

The Role of the School Librarian

A traditional solution for informing administrators about school library programs is through one-on-one contact with school librarians (Baule 2004; Hartzell 2002; McNeil and Wilson 1999). In this scenario the school librarian raises the administrator's awareness through his or her actions on behalf of the library media program and through interactions with the administrator (Levitov 2009). This strategy is corroborated in an interview conducted by school librarian Carl Harvey (2007), where his principal establishes how he came to learn about school libraries and the value of the program through the work of Harvey. This on-the-job training has worked as a way of informing the principal and advocating for the program and should not be undervalued by the school librarian.

In survey findings by Alexander, Smith, and Carey (2003) they report, "The building level professional is the only one with the opportunity for day-to-day influence on the perceptions of the principal" (13). It is important for school librarians to realize that they must serve as a central source for educating school administrators about school library programs on a daily basis (Levitov 2009). After participating in an online course, "School Library Advocacy for Administrators," school administrators indicated that regarding the success of the school librarian, "personality counts, leadership is key, advocacy is essential and communication is imperative" (Levitov 2009). In his book, Snyder (2000), a school principal, states,

The survival of school libraries depends on the commitment of its stakeholders, and the extent of that commitment rests with its professionals: they hold the key to their destiny; they have the power to shape decisions. They can—and must—sell their programs to critical decision makers. (xvii)

The school librarian should take on a leadership role in communicating with administrators about school library programs in a way that is beneficial to the work of the administrator. This communication must resonate with administrators' needs by using their language, linking to their agenda, reflecting their priorities. School principal Steven M. Baule (2004) suggests that school librarians should "show (not tell) administrators how the school library program can help them" (24). He says that the goals of the school library program should be linked to the school improvement plan and that requests from the school librarian should be framed in this context. Baule also emphasizes that the school librarian should not focus on which school library/information-learning standards "[they] will meet but what students will be able to do that they could not do previously" (24). Allison Zmuda (2006) refers to this idea when she asks school librarians where their authority comes from—"authority to work with students in a rigorous, relevant, and consistent manner." It is the proof of student learning, through assessment and evidence-based practice, that becomes a powerful tool for advocacy.

Baule goes on to say that school librarians should be in regular communication with their administrators, they should have a presence on school committees, and they should serve the entire school community. As a result "the school library media program will gain stature through [their] strategic involvement in all aspects of the school" (Baule 2004, 25).

Aligning with the advice of Baule, Carl Harvey stresses the need to align the agenda of the school library program with that of the principal so that it ultimately becomes part of the principal's agenda. He summarizes with the statement that

it is key for us to take the time and energy to review the principal's agenda and the established school goals while advancing our own agenda.... Advocacy is getting someone else to share your message and tell your story. If our story includes how we are helping our principal improve student achievement and reach the goals on his or her agenda, then our principal is quite likely ... to be telling our story to many others! (Harvey 2007)

Communication by the school librarian with the building administrator is a crucial part of advocacy leadership. It is a necessary step in building partnerships and educating stakeholders—ultimately turning them into informed school library advocates.

Background Knowledge Equals Impact

According to Alexander, Smith, and Cary's 2003 Kentucky study, fewer than 10 percent of the principals responding had taken a college course including content related to school librarian and principal collaboration. Yet principals that had participated in such course work "rated the library media center significantly higher, 7.00 on a 10-point scale, than the principals who had not taken a course, who rated the value of the library media center at 4.97" (Alexander, Smith, and Carey 2003).

The research indicates those who have more background knowledge about school libraries have a more favorable view of programs. Thus finding ways to educate those intricately connected to school libraries is a worthy goal. And since day-to-day interaction between the school librarian and the administrator remains one of the most reliable methods, it is essential that school librarians take on the leadership role for communicating with administrators as a first step toward building understanding, garnering support, and growing advocacy. This leads to stakeholder advocacy.

Through an Institute for Museum and Library Services grant, Mansfield University's School Library and Information Technologies online graduate school has been "offering an educational option for school administrators to learn the background, research and skills necessary to maximize their library media programs" (Kachel 2006). The online course work requires 15 hours of participation from the principals.

In a study conducted with 13 administrators that participated in the course during two different sessions, the administrators

provided examples of how they changed their perceptions of library media programs. They indicated how the Mansfield online course provided information that gave them new ideas and concepts about school library media that they did not previously know. They also suggested that they changed their actions toward their library programs and began to make changes related to their action plans. (Levitov 2009)

The background information gained by these administrators appears to have made a difference in how they perceived their school library programs and to have impacted their actions involving the school library.

Short of getting principals to take an online course like that offered by Mansfield, Kachel (2006) suggests steps that school librarians can take to help educate their principals:

1.) Start by doing some homework, use resources like Gary Hartzell's book *Building Influence for the School Librarian* (2003); 2.) Complete the AASL Program Assessment rubric (AASL 1999, 35–51), and base self-evaluation on the rubric, communicating the plan with the principal (it is still applicable today); 3.) Meet regularly with the principal to discuss goals; have a clear agenda with a time limit; 4.) Report progress and share summaries of current research whenever possible; 5.) Assess where the principal needs more background information and provide it; 6.) Build rapport with the principal and communicate on an ongoing basis. (Kachel, 2006)

THE IMPORTANCE OF LANGUAGE

School librarians should be cognizant of language used when communicating with stakeholders. According to Whelan and Ishizuka,

In order for today's librarians to succeed in the profession, they need to completely overhaul the way they conduct business by reaching out to all educators, from federal and state agencies to departments of education and technology experts. [They must] speak a common language with their colleagues. (2005)

This requires clarity in what is said—to assure that it is understood, as well as to show why it is important and how it connects to the priorities of those listening:

The common language of library media specialists should not be abandoned. Instead, library media professionals need to see through the eyes of those with whom they want to communicate and include terms that resonate with them. They need to consciously embed and use terms and language that can build connections and communicate shared agendas. (Levitov 2008)

The AASL's *Standards for the 21st-Century Learner* (2007) is a perfect example of language alignment. By using the language found in the Partnership for 21st Century Skills (P21) initiative, AASL has done a brilliant job of capitalizing on common language and beliefs and making the connection through the AASL standards document. In a comparison of P21 and AASL standards, Formanack (2008) emphasizes, "The new standards reflect many of the Partnership for 21st Century Skills of critical thinking and problem solving, creativity and innovation, and communication and collaboration" (30). She goes on to state, "Substantive discussion about the language in both of these documents is needed to change the culture of library media centers" (Formanack 2008).

This type of discourse must lead the effort to build an advocacy plan that will reach out and involve others. These types of connections must be part of leading advocacy efforts.

ADVOCACY IN ACTION

Involving Others

Often, school librarians take on the advocacy effort and deliver it through one-way messages that can be construed as self-serving. Catherine Byers makes an argument for enlisting the choir, stressing that the school librarian "can't be the lone proponent of [their] school library program. Other voices—parents, coworkers, and students—must all play their respective roles in communicating the value of a great school library media center" (2005b).

Creating an action plan that targets ways to speak to and enlist these key players is an important part of advocacy. Starting a plan may involve identifying what is important to each target group and providing services to match their priorities. Asking them what they need and want and finding ways to deliver is in itself advocacy. These goodwill gestures can serve as powerful steps in building advocates. As these audiences see the value and importance of the school library, their voices can reach administrators, community members, school board members, and legislators, providing a much more powerful message than a single school librarian can ever deliver.

The importance of winning friends and influencing people cannot be underestimated; both are important components of building the groundwork for advocacy and should be everyday efforts. Byers offers simple examples, such as providing parents with checkout cards so they can use school library resources to meet parenting or literacy needs, continually communicating with parents about how the library helps their children learn, involving teachers in collection development or identifying services the library can provide, finding out what students want and need from the library and making it happen (2005b).

Friends groups are another way to build advocates. Rocco Staino, a school librarian from North Salem, New York, shares the importance of taking the time and effort to cultivate these friendships (2007). He suggests that school librarians should make use of the national organization Friends of Libraries U.S.A. (http://www.folusa.org) to build a group made up of "teachers, parents, community members, and students as core advocates" (Staino 2007, 43). Friends of Libraries U.S.A. has materials geared specifically to friends groups for school libraries and guidelines for determining the main purpose of such a group. These groups can advocate for issues related to school library funding, recruitment of volunteers, or the need for quality school libraries. They can speak out against funding cuts, or they can send representatives to lobbying days. In the end, a friends group for the school library can serve as a powerful advocate.

Action Planning

Advance planning for advocacy is essential. Catherine Byers points out, "How will we know if we have made progress if we don't know where we are going?" (2005a).

Her approach is to create "measurable goals" for herself, the library assistant, and the principal to sign and periodically review throughout the year for progress, as well as to review at the end of the year for evaluation (Byers 2006). Byers's approach turned into a three-year planning process that helped "alter the focus of our goal setting. Rather than concentrate on what I thought we needed to do, I instead tried to focus on what our patrons wanted out of the library media program" (2005a, 45). This is an example of meeting the needs of the stakeholders, by knowing their priorities and what is important to them and linking their agendas to that of the school library program within a plan of action.

Having a Web Presence

The online presence of the school library is an essential component for the school library of the present. As Catherine Byers points out, "Developing a good public relations image requires projecting a positive impression of our school library media program as well as winning the confidence and approval of our clientele" (2006). Many open source tools (e.g., Web sites, wikis, blogs, twitters) allow the school librarian to make ongoing, up-to-date connections, to provide services, as well as to communicate with stakeholders in a timely manner. Whatever the tool, it is important to have the school library represented virtually. That representation reflects currency and ongoing efforts to communicate and meet the needs of the target audiences. The school library Web 2.0 presence is the perfect opportunity to share stories from students and staff related to the school library, to make connections to learning, and to provide resources and tools 24/7.

Grant Writing

Involving others in the process of grant writing for the school library is a way to gain input from teachers, administrators, parents, students, or business people (Baxter 2007). Grant writing is also a means of obtaining funding for special initiatives for library program planning or collection development. Involvement by others can serve as a way to further educate them about the school library program and gain informed voices of support. Grant writing can become a tool for advocacy by building collaborative partnerships and funding initiatives that are high priority for stakeholders involved in the process. As Pat Franklin and Claire Stephens (school librarians in Orlando, Florida) share, "Helping teachers write grants is a great way to foster collaboration and open doors to get to know them better. The outcome could . . . gain materials for both the classroom and the library media center" (2008, 44). It can also foster advocates through personal, one-on-one advocacy.

Getting a Seat at the Table . . .

Members of both the Massachusetts and Wisconsin school library associations used strategies of long-term planning with group advocacy to ensure that school librarians were involved in their state initiatives for the P21 program (Partnership for 21st Century Skills). As Sandy Kelly explains, Massachusetts school librarians deliberately worked to build advocacy through "persistence, education, and frequent reassessment" (2008, 23). Thus, when they learned their state was interested in becoming a P21 state, they were well prepared to initiate involvement and get a seat at the table for planning the initiative. The same was true in Wisconsin—"library media specialists and technology leaders around the state were already working on implementation of these skills" (2008, 28). Through their group advocacy efforts, school librarians were able to have a part in P21 planning.

Evidence of Student Learning

Another powerful form of advocacy is providing evidence of student learning in the school library. As Vi Harada points out, "Library media programs are frequently on the chopping block when school budgets shrink" (2006, 25). When budget cuts are imminent, school decision-makers "seek to support programs that demonstrate positive student growth in areas of high need" (2006, 25). She offers a way in which school librarians can provide this sort of evidence, through *evidence folders*, a holding place for recording lessons and proof of student learning through student work and assessment data.

As Harada describes it, an "evidence folder is a way to communicate what students learn through the library media center to other members of the school community" (2008, 27). Proof of student learning serves as a most powerful form of advocacy, because it establishes the important role that school librarians play in educating students. As Zmuda and Harada put forth, "Good business [in the school library] is work (instructional activities and assessments) that develops student learning around the goals that are most important" (2008, 42).

Legislative Action

Emily Sheketoff, executive director of the Washington, D.C., office of the American Library Association, argues that school librarians should get involved advocating for funding for school libraries. She defines advocacy as "simply voicing your support for your library media center and encouraging others to do the same" (2006, 50). Sheketoff contends, "The more people who speak out, the stronger the voices for libraries will be" (51). It takes a village for successful advocacy efforts—an example of group advocacy.

Reaching out to local legislators is a first step in building legislative advocacy. As Diane Chen states, "When you invite [legislators] to visit your school, you take the big issues and make them local; you help them understand the links between state and national actions" (2007, 47). Chen goes on to suggest that the school librarian should get to know their elected officials, and she offers the following guideposts for school librarians to build their political voice:

- Find out what is important to state and national legislators and connect those interests to programs in local and school libraries;
- Know their staff and keep contact information handy;
- Invite them to your school to read to students or welcome parents to special events;
- Take pictures and prepare op-eds about your program, share your success stories and how you meet the learning needs of students;
- Figure out ways to advance their causes while linking to your agenda;
- Communicate often and share student work and positive stories;

- Offer to answer questions about school libraries and find the answers when you aren't sure;
- Call to voice your support of a bill;
- Get others to speak up for issues;
- Use the ALAL-WO [American Library Association Legislative-Washington Office] Legislative Action Center to stay abreast of school library related issues and for contacting your senators and members of Congress. (2007)

Building rapport with government representatives before times of crisis is one of the wisest forms of advocacy. Then, when the time comes to communicate about an important issue, the school librarian will have an established image with legislators and will have personalized him- or herself and the program. The efforts of the Pennsylvania School Librarians Association legislative committee echo Chen's outreach efforts. This association has developed an organized effort, made possible with the help of retired school librarians, to orchestrate visits by legislators to schools—complete with media coverage and follow-up thank you notes (Kachel 2008). Both examples are proactive, building connections and relationships that can be useful when critical issues arise.

The legislative effort on the behalf of school libraries by the Spokane Moms is the ultimate example of stakeholder advocacy. "Fueled by the knowledge of what closed library doors meant to their own seven children, these Spokane moms called school district personnel and school board members, and finally went to their local legislators in an attempt to reverse library media center closures" (Kaaland 2008). The ongoing Washington political effort was due to the combined efforts of the Washington Library Media Association advocacy members and the Washington Coalition for School Libraries and Information Technology founded by the Spokane Moms.

Legislative advocacy takes dedication and reflects effort over great spans of time. This is illustrated in the case of the Washington efforts, as well as in the recent example of 10 years' worth of legislative efforts in Ohio culminating in the passage of HB1 with language requiring "licensed" librarians and media specialists in Ohio schools (Logan 2009).

WAITING FOR THE TIPPING POINT—MYTH OR POSSIBILITY?

The "hundredth monkey phenomenon" became very popular in the early 1980s when it was presented as scientific fact by one Lyall Watson, a botanist, zoologist, biologist, anthropologist, and ethnologist. Watson described the phenomenon in two pages in his book *Lifetide* (Simon and Schuster 1979), as the "remarkable and supernatural behavior of primates" in Japan—a phenomenon he loosely tied to five articles written by Japanese primatologists (Frazier 1991). The myth took on a life of its own before finally being debunked by the end of the 1980s. As Maureen O'Hara pointed out, the speed at which the myth was passed along "makes a far better case study of the phenomenon [of critical mass] that the monkey research putatively demonstrates" (O'Hara as cited in Frazier, 1991).

While the "hundredth monkey" myth could not be substantiated, the concept of critical mass gained more recent attention through contemporary studies in the context of such things as education, crime, disease, and advertisement (Gladwell 1996; Gladwell 2002). In his book *The Tipping Point* (2002), Malcolm Gladwell described the tipping point as "that magic moment when an idea, trend, or social behavior crosses a threshold, tips, and spreads like wildfire" (from back cover). According to Word Spy, an online dictionary of newly coined words, "tipping point" means

in epidemiology, the concept that small changes will have little or no effect on a system until a critical mass is reached. Then a further small change "tips" the system and a large effect is observed. ("Tipping Point")

School library professionals have been hoping for a tipping point or a critical mass—a point when school administrators and others understand the potential of the school library program within the educational setting, resulting in support and appreciation for school librarians and school library programs. As with the hundredth monkey case, a critical mass does not appear to be waiting in the wings for school library programs. But there are ways for school librarians to lead the advocacy efforts.

Through personal, one-on-one advocacy and group advocacy, informed advocates can be created who are involved in the process and equipped to speak up for and defend school library programs and school librarians. Group advocacy can be orchestrated by school librarians and/or stakeholders, and information can be provided for target audiences, linking to the needs and desires of each and raising awareness so that they too will become involved and advocate for library programs.

CONCLUSION

There is a great deal of power in advocacy, and it takes the leadership of every school librarian to build this type of support. This advocacy must be based on a shared vision of what a school library is and should be, a vision that reflects the needs of the twenty-first-century learner, teacher, and school. Allison Zmuda (2006) sent out a wake-up call to school librarians about self-serving advocacy, summarized as "rhetorical contention based on the unabashedly biased viewpoint of those professionals that seem to have the most to gain" (19). She and Ross Todd challenge school librarians instead to bridge the gaps of what is believed important about school libraries and *show* the importance through actions—demonstrating outcomes that occur *because of* strong school libraries through evidence of student learning (Zmuda 2006; Todd 2009). In the end, the largest challenges for advocacy planning are (1) re-imaging school libraries in the minds of stakeholders and, in many instances, school librarians and (2) taking on the challenge of evidence-based practice—showing the role of the school librarian and the program in student learning. These two challenges will impact the attitudes of students, parents, teachers, administrators, legislators, school board members, and all stakeholders, because it will formulate how they define school libraries. This definition will in turn determine the future of school libraries.

School libraries must be promoted, supported, and defended every day, and school librarians must lead the effort. This effort must be relentless and must be the essence of an ongoing advocacy plan. Just think, if every school librarian practiced advocacy, one-on-one, home grown, day to day, what effect it would have on the state of school libraries everywhere? Just think, if every school librarian would reach out to his or her legislators and communicate with them over time and advocate for specific legislation related to school libraries, what effect would it have on school libraries everywhere? Just think, if every school librarian communicated with students, teachers, and administrators in a way that resonated with them, what effect would it have on school libraries everywhere? What if every school librarian gathered evidence-based assessment of student learning and shared the information with stakeholders; how would the image of school libraries change?

Although there is no cookie-cutter solution to advocacy for school libraries, there are strategies and guidelines that can be incorporated into plans that fit the locale. The leadership of the school librarian is instrumental in attaining the AASL definition of advocacy as an "on-going process of building partnerships so that others will act for and with you, turning passive support into educated action for the library media program ... matching the agenda and priorities of stakeholders" ("Advocacy"). The plan for advocacy must be developed and implemented by individuals, as well as groups, over time. It is a combined, many-faceted effort that will result in the creation of advocates for the school library profession and in the creation of school library programs that will be sustainable.

REFERENCES

Alexander, L., C. Smith, and J. Carey. 2003. Education reform and the school library media specialist: Perceptions of principals. *Knowledge Quest* 32 (1): 10–13.

American Association of School Librarians. Advocacy. http://www.ala.org/ala/mgrps/divs/aasl/aaslissues/aasladvocacy/definitions.cfm (accessed September 12, 2009).

———. 1999. *A planning guide for information power: Building partnerships for learning.* Chicago: AASL.

Baule, Steven M. 2004. Politips for school librarians: Or, working with your administrator. *Knowledge Quest* 33 (1): 24–25.

Baxter, Veanna. 2007. Library media advocacy through grant writing. *School Library Media Activities Monthly* 24 (2): 45–48.

Byers, Catherine. 2005a. Chart your course. *School Library Media Activities Monthly* 22 (1): 45–46.

———. 2005b. Enlist the choir. *School Library Media Activities Monthly* 22 (2): 47–48.

———. 2006. Plugged in @ your library®. *School Library Media Activities Monthly* 22 (9): 49–50.

Campbell, B. S. 1994. High school principal roles and implementation themes for mainstreaming information literacy instruction. Doctoral dissertation. University of Connecticut.

Chen, Diane R. 2007. The importance of the library media specialist as a political voice. *School Library Media Activities Monthly* 23 (10): 46–48.

Formanack, Gail. 2008. The importance of language: The Partnership for 21st Century Skills and AASL standards. *School Library Media Activities Monthly* 25 (1): 28–30.

Franklin, Pat, and Claire Gatrell Stephens. 2008. Gaining skills to write winning grants. *School Library Media Activities Monthly* 25 (3): 43–44.

Frazier, Kendrick. 1991. *The hundredth monkey and other paradigms of the paranormal.* Amherst, NY: Prometheus Books.

Gladwell, Malcolm. 1996. *The tipping point.* The New Yorker, 72 (14): 32–38.

———. 2002. *The tipping point.* New York: Little, Brown.

Harada, Violet H. 2006. Building evidence folders for learning through library media centers. *School Library Media Activities Monthly* 23 (3): 25–30.

Hartzell, G. 2002. The principals' perceptions of school libraries and teacher-librarians. *School Libraries Worldwide* 8 (1): 92–110.

———. 2003. *Building influence for the school librarian* (2nd ed.). Worthington, OH: Linworth.

Harvey, Carl, II. 2007. Aligning school library media and principal agendas. *School Library Media Activities Monthly* 23 (9): 48–49.

Haycock, Ken. 2004. Sad, so sad, it's not about us. *Teacher Librarian* 31 (3): 6.

Johns, Sara Kelly. 2007. Advocacy: AASL puts the puzzle together. *Knowledge Quest* 35 (1): 4–5.

Kaaland, Christie. 2008. Making history on a shoestring: The story of the Spokane Moms. *School Library Media Activities Monthly* 24 (9): 45–46.

———. 2009. A campaign of gratitude. *School Library Media Activities Monthly* 25 (9): 52–53.

Kachel, Debra E. 2006. Educating your principal. *School Library Media Activities Monthly* 23 (3): 48–50.

———. 2008. PSLA legislators@your library campaign. *Teacher Librarian* 36 (2): 15–16.

Kelly, Sandy. 2008. Getting a seat at the table—an ongoing effort. *School Library Media Activities Monthly* 25 (3): 23–28.

Levitov, Deborah. 2007. One library media specialist's journey to understanding advocacy: A tale of transformation. *School Library Media Activities Monthly* 36 (1): 28–31.

———. 2008. Language—communication or jargon? *School Library Media Activities Monthly* 24 (5): 45–46.

———. 2009. Perspectives of school administrators related to school library media programs after participating in an online course, "School Library Advocacy for Administrators." Doctoral dissertation. University of Missouri–Columbia.

Logan, Debra Kay. 2009. Making the impossible dream come true: The Ohio quest to serve students. *Teacher Librarian* 37 (1): 40–42.

McNeil, A., and P. P. Wilson. 1999–2000. Preparing principals for the leadership role in library media centers. *Applied Educational Research Journal* 12 (2): 21–27.

Oberg, D., L. Hay, and J. Henri. 2000. The role of the principal in an information literate school community: Design and Administration of an International Research Project. *School Library Media Research* 3. American Library Association, Document ID: 202793. http://www.ala.org/ala/mgrps/divs/aasl/aaslpubsandjournals/slmrb/slmrcontents/volume32000/principal.cfm (accessed January 11, 2009).

O'Neal, A. J. 2004. Administrators' and media specialists' perceptions of the roles of media specialists in the schools' instructional programs: Implications for instructional administration. *Journal of Education for Library and Information Science* 45 (4): 286–306.

Rose, K. E. 2002. Profiles in success: The leadership role of the principal as initiator, facilitator, and sustainer of change in Blue Ribbon Elementary Schools in Illinois. Doctoral dissertation. Northern Illinois University at Dekalb.

Shannon, D. 2002. Education and competencies of school library media specialists: A review of the literature. American Library Association, Document ID: 202809. http://www.ala.org/ala/mgrps/divs/aasl/aaslpubsandjournals/slmrb/slmrcontents/volume52002/shannon.cfm (accessed November 20, 2009).

Sheketoff, Emily. 2006. Federal legislative action: Key to your library media center's success. *School Library Media Activities Monthly* 23 (4): 50–51.

Smith, Annette R. 2008. Library media specialists making an impact. *School Library Media Activities Monthly* 25 (3): 27–29.

Snyder, T. 2000. *Getting lead-bottomed administrators excited about school library media centers.* Westport, CT: Libraries Unlimited.

Staino, Rocco. 2007. Friends groups: Finding their way into library media centers. *School Library Media Activities Monthly* 24 (3): 43–45.

Stripling, Barbara. 2007. The dance of leadership and advocacy. *Knowledge Quest* 36: 54–55.

Todd, Ross. 2009. *To be or not to be: Reimagining school libraries.* Presented by Ross Todd at Treasure Mountain Research Forum #15, Charlotte, N.C., November 2009.

Watson, Lyall. 1986. Lifetide. New York: Simon and Schuster.

Whelan, Debra Lau, and Kathy Ishizuka. 2005. Educational leaders gather in NYC to resolve most pressing obstacles to learning. *School Library Journal* (April 1). http://www .schoollibraryjournal.com/article/CAS514027.html (accessed July 19, 2009).

Word Spy. Tipping point. http://www.wordspy.com/words/tippingpoint.asp.

Zmuda, Allison. 2006. Where does your authority come from?: Empowering the library media specialist as a true partner in student achievement. *School Library Media Activities Monthly* 23 (1): 19–22.

Zmuda, Allison, and Violet H. Harada. 2008. Reframing the library media specialist as a learning specialist. *School Library Media Activities Monthly* 24 (8): 42–47.

ADDITIONAL READING

American Association of School Librarians. 2007. *Standards for the 21st-century learner.* American Library Association.

———. 2007. *Standards for the 21st-century learner in action.* American Association of School Librarians.

———. 2009. *Empowering learners: Guidelines for school library media programs.* American Association of School Librarians.

Fontichiaro, Kristin. 2009. *21st-century learning in school libraries.* Libraries Unlimited.

Hall-Ellis, Sylvia D. 2003. *Grants for school libraries.* Libraries Unlimited.

Harada, Violet H., and Joan M. Yoshina. 2005. *Assessing learning: Librarians and teachers as partners.* Libraries Unlimited.

Haycock, Ken, and Wendy Newman. Forthcoming. *School library advocacy: Creating a common agenda.* Libraries Unlimited.

Helm, Judy Harris, and Amanda Helm. 2006. *Building support for your school: How to use children's work to show learning.* New York: Teachers College Press, 2006.

Hughes-Hassell, Sandra, and Violet H. Harada. 2007. *School reform and the school library media specialist.* Libraries Unlimited.

Kuhlthau, Carol C., Leslie K. Maniotes, and Ann K. Caspari. 2007. *Guided inquiry: Learning in the 21st Century.* Libraries Unlimited.

Schuckett, Sandy. 2004. *Political advocacy for school librarians: You have the power.* Linworth.

Siess, Judith A., and Jonathan Lorig. 2007. *Out front with Stephen Abram: A guide for information leaders.* ALA Editions.

Stephens, Claire G. 2007. *Library 101: A handbook for the school library media specialist.* Libraries Unlimited.

Toor, Ruth, and Hilda K. Weisburg. 2006. *New on the job: A school library media specialist's guide to success.* ALA Editions.

Vance, Anita L., and Robbie Nickel, eds. 2007. *Assessing student learning in the school library media center.* ALA Editions.

Zmuda, Allison, and Violet H. Harada. 2008. *Librarians as learning specialists: Meeting the learning imperative for the 21st century.* Libraries Unlimited.

4

Intellectual Freedom: Leadership to Preserve Minors' Rights in School Library Media Programs

Helen R. Adams

DEFINING LEADERSHIP

One definition of leadership is "the art of motivating a group of people to act towards achieving a common goal" (Ward, "Leadership"). Leaders in schools have traditionally been the district administrators, principals, directors of instruction, technology coordinators, and district library media supervisors; their leadership is based on position. There are also *informal leaders* such as some library media specialists who, by their strength of personality or belief in a goal and by effective communication skills, inspire or encourage others to acknowledge their ideas. Informal leadership can create its own political influence to encourage positive change.

To be a leader in the area of *intellectual freedom* in a K–12 educational community requires the general leadership skills described earlier in this volume. More specifically, a school library media specialist must possess:

- A vision of the broad concepts of intellectual freedom
- Knowledge of the documents that define and defend intellectual freedom, including the First Amendment, court decisions supporting minors' rights, and policy statements of the American Library Association
- Strategies for how intellectual freedom principles are translated into practical action to preserve the legal rights of children and young adults
- Ethical fitness to acknowledge that personal beliefs should not interfere with professional duties, as stated in the *Code of Ethics of the American Library Association*
- Character traits such as enthusiasm, honesty, courage, persistence, and the mental toughness to persevere in response to resistance, conflict, and personal attacks
- Communication skills to inspire others to acknowledge, support, and collaborate to protect the intellectual freedom of students

School library professionals have a responsibility to lead in many areas, but intellectual freedom requires a special type of leadership. It involves advocating for minors' First Amendment rights by using case law, American Library Association policy statements, and the power of persuasion to support those rights. It requires knowledge of federal and state laws that impact students' access to information in all formats and that protect their privacy when using library resources. It incorporates core values of librarianship such as access, privacy and confidentiality, democracy, diversity, service, education, and professionalism (American Library Association [ALA], "Core Values"). Defending intellectual freedom requires the courage to protect and educate the school and broader local community about the rights of students using the school library media center.

LEADERSHIP TO PROVIDE ACCESS TO INFORMATION

The First Amendment guarantees "freedom of speech," which has been interpreted by the courts as more than verbal communication. In *Board of Education v. Pico*, a plurality of the justices recognized that minors have a "right to receive information" whether the information is in print, non-print, or other format. The majority of leadership responsibilities for the library media specialist fall within the categories of providing access to library media program resources and protecting that access.

THE SELECTION POLICY

The selection of resources for the library media collection is a major part of ensuring minors' right to receive information. One of the first acts of leadership by the school library professional is to determine if the district or school has a written, board-approved instructional and library materials selection policy, with procedures to provide a formal process for reviewing any materials about which a concern has been raised. This policy is the *legal basis* for selection and reconsideration of all instructional and library materials and establishes that all resources are acquired under a standard set of criteria.

If no instructional materials selection policy is in place, the school library media specialist must encourage the principal and other administrators to develop such a policy. Collaboration is critical when developing an instructional materials selection policy. The most effective selection policy is developed with input from a broad representation of members of the school community, including school library professionals, teachers, administrators, students, and parent and board of education representatives. Including the many stakeholders in the policy creation process assures smooth implementation and support for the document. When completed, the policy will reflect the educational goals and objectives of the district or school and guide the selection of resources to serve its unique student population and support the curriculum. The policy will also protect students' right to receive information by stopping the removal of legally acquired library materials without due process.

SELECTION OF LIBRARY MEDIA PROGRAM RESOURCES

Although the board of education or governing authority of the institution is legally responsible for the resources used within a school, it delegates the actual selection of library resources to its professional school library personnel. The school library professional provides leadership in implementing the selection policy, selecting materials based on official criteria, and following the procedures within the policy.

Selecting school library resources is one of the most critical responsibilities of a library media specialist. Selection can be controversial because protection of children and youth is a large part of the culture of the United States. The school library professional selects library resources to support the curriculum and provide for the reading and information interests of students. It is no small task to select resources meeting the district selection policy, which may include these criteria:

- appropriate for the age, interests, emotional development, ability levels, learning styles, and social development of the students for whom the resources are intended including students with disabilities
- accurate in terms of content and authority of the author
- free of bias and stereotyping (e.g., sexism, racism)
- reflect the pluralistic nature of a global society
- represent the various religious, ethnic, gender, and cultural groups and their contributions to American heritage
- depict diverse points of view on controversial topics (Adams 2008, 40)

Using these criteria, as well as others within the selection policy, may result in the acquisition of resources that will cause an individual to express a concern or file a written complaint based on protecting his/her child or all children from the information, language, images, or perspectives within the resource. A library professional demonstrates leadership during the selection process by unequivocally using the official criteria to *guide his/her selection* and, in the event of a challenge, using the policy's same criteria to *defend the selection*. Every resource chosen should be directly defensible because it met one or more of the selection criteria prior to purchase, and a conscious effort should be made to match the prospective resource with as many criteria as possible.

During the selection process, the school library media specialist must remain conscious of the potential for *self-censorship*. Not selecting a book or other resource because of fear that someone may challenge an item on the basis of its sexual content, objectionable language, or violence, or because of personal bias or religious or political convictions, is self-censorship. Former school library media specialist Pat Scales defines self-censorship this way:

Some may argue that librarians are merely selecting what they feel are the best books for kids and that it's not censorship. But the key factor is one's intent. A trained media specialist is expected to choose a range of titles that best suits the curriculum and meets the reading needs of students—and that involves making judgment calls. But if you reject a book just because of its subject matter or if you think that it would cause you some problems, then that's self-censorship. And that's going against professional ethics. (Whelan 2009)

According to Susan Patron, author of Newbery award-winner *The Higher Power of Lucky*, "In a way, self-censorship is more frightening than outright banning or removal of challenged material because these incidents tend to 'slip under the radar' " (Whelan 2009).

Figure 4.1
Self-Censorship Checklist

Has your library ever . . .

Not purchased material because a review or publisher's catalog indicated that it was for "mature readers," had explicit language or illustrations, or might be controversial?

___ yes ___ no

Not purchased a popular book because it might be unpopular with parents or pressure groups in the community?

___ yes ___ no

Not purchased material because of the origin, background or views of the author?

___ yes ___ no

Not purchased sex instruction materials from a conservative religious point of view because a staff member found them to be personally offensive?

___ yes ___ no

Not purchased magazines, videos, rock or rap music, or books because "they are so popular they might be stolen?"

___ yes ___ no

Not purchased material concerning minorities because "no one in our community is like that?"

___ yes ___ no

Not purchased a popular recording because of controversial lyrics or cover art?

___ yes ___ no

Purchased a potentially controversial book, but put it in the Adult collection rather than the Young Adult collection for which it was intended?

___ yes ___ no

Reviewed a potentially controversial item and recommended that it not be purchased because of lack of literary merit, even though other non-controversial materials in the collection also lacked literary merit?

___ yes ___ no

Checked a magazine for potentially controversial content, language, or illustrations, and then restricted access or removed it from the collection?

___ yes ___ no

Labeled controversial materials in order to "warn" or prejudice possible users?

___ yes ___ no

Restricted children's use of certain sections of the library (e.g., adult reading room), types of materials (e.g., videos), or services (e.g., interlibrary loan)?

____ yes ____ no

Placed potentially controversial materials in restricted areas so that patrons are required to request them?

____ yes ____ no

Denied library use to someone because of his or her age, gender, sexual orientation, ethnicity, political, or religious views?

____ yes ____ no

Set policies based on video or music producers' ratings to restrict access even though local ordinances don't prohibit use by minors?

____ yes ____ no

Responded to a challenge and removed objectionable material without going through a formal reconsideration of materials process?

____ yes ____ no

Cooperated in violating the right to privacy of your users by providing unauthorized access to their library records?

____ yes ____ no

Prohibited use of your meeting room or bulletin board to groups whose views you disagreed with?

____ yes ____ no

If you answered yes to any of these questions, it's time to review your intellectual freedom practices!

Reprinted with permission from the Intellectual Freedom Committee of the New York Library Association.

A leader does not engage in self-censorship. How can a school library professional protect against self-censorship? Be conscious of the *Code of Ethics of the American Library Association* during selection. Article VII states, "We distinguish between our personal convictions and professional duties and do not allow our personal beliefs to interfere with fair representation of the aims of our institutions or the provision of access to their information resources" (ALA 2007). Discuss your concerns with others in the profession. Megan Schliesman, a librarian at the Cooperative Children's Book Center at the University of Wisconsin–Madison advises,

If fear is at the root of self-censoring behavior, talk about those fears and weigh them against reality. No matter how certain someone is that a book or other item will offend someone, no one knows for certain when—or over what—a challenge may arise. And no library can function

effectively if any member of the staff is fearful of making selection decisions. Everyone responsible for materials selection needs to understand their policy: how it supports and empowers them
to serve their community, be it students and staff in a school, or the citizens of a community.
(Adams 2008, 49)

School library media specialists who are leaders are proactive and ardent about providing access to a diverse collection. They involve the principal, teachers, students, and
parents in the selection process. They maintain a cordial, collaborative relationship
with the principal. Annually they review the selection policy and selection criteria with
the principal, report the current needs for curriculum support, summarize the types of
fiction and nonfiction that may be purchased for student personal reading, and encourage the principal to recommend books and other resources for acquisition. When new
materials arrive, the library professional alerts the principal and faculty through email
or via a "new resources" list on the library's Web site. She or he arranges for the principal and faculty to preview new items prior to their being circulated to students, offers
refreshments, and converses about the new acquisitions. Equally important, the librarian also sets aside personal biases and orders materials containing ideas and viewpoints
with which he or she does not agree. To protect against self-censorship, the school
media professional uses a tool such as the New York Library Association's "Self-
Censorship Checklist" (Figure 4.1, p. 46) to remain within ethical selection practices.

LEADERSHIP TO PROTECT ACCESS TO INFORMATION

One of the most serious circumstances in which leadership is required by a school
library media specialist is when an oral or written complaint is made against a library
resource. Those who bring an oral concern or formal written challenge have that right
to do so, and their opinions deserve respect. While library and school staff may not
agree with the request to remove or restrict the resource, a district's reconsideration
process sets in motion another evaluation of the resource, and one of the school library
professional's *unwritten* responsibilities will be to help ensure that the process is
followed.

PREPARING FOR A CHALLENGE

Leaders plan ahead and prepare for challenging situations. They are proactive and
reach out to build a coalition of like-minded individuals and groups who have similar
goals. From the first day on the job, the library media specialist should begin to take
the following steps to prepare for a challenge:

- Inquire whether the district has a school board-approved materials selection policy that
  includes a formal process for reconsidering challenged library resources.
- Verify that the selection policy is current with respect to such issues as selection of Web sites to
  be included as links on the school library's site and criteria for acquiring multimedia resources
  in new formats (Wolf 2008, 10–11). Talk to the principal about updating the policy if necessary,
  and volunteer to serve on the committee.
- Discuss and clarify with administrators any steps or responsibilities in the official reconsideration process that may not be clear.

- Post the materials selection policy and the reconsideration process on the school library media program Web site. Include downloadable copies of the district's form for requesting reconsideration of library materials.
- Ensure that administrators, teachers, students, parents, and extended families understand how school library media program resources are selected and the criteria used, by such means as staff development, parent presentations, and newsletter articles.
- Add an electronic form to the library Web site that allows administrators, teachers, students, and parents to suggest new materials for the collection.
- Work with the principal and other stakeholders to create a selection policy if one is not in place, and seek its formal approval by the governing body.
- Confer with the principal about establishing a schedule for regular review of all library media program and information access policies, such as an acceptable use policy, to identify areas that need revision.

Leaders build relationships with all stakeholders through their visibility and participation in school activities. Relationship-building opportunities include serving on curriculum or other in-school committees, collaborating with faculty members on student projects, offering professional development programs, participating in student-focused activities such as homecoming, attending extracurricular events, and sponsoring a library open house during parent-teacher conferences. Another very simple way to establish rapport with teachers is to eat with various groups of faculty members during different lunch periods. The result will be that faculty get to know the school library professional as a person and professional colleague, and the reverse is also true. Although adding to the library media specialist's already lengthy "to do" list, each outreach activity offers a unique opportunity to establish informal exchanges with colleagues, administrators, students, and parents. Those connections over a period of time build a positive professional reputation for the school library media specialist in the school community and may garner allies or at least respectful adversaries if a formal challenge to library resources occurs.

ORAL COMPLAINTS

Not everyone who has a concern about a book or other library resource wants to remove it from the collection. Some individuals simply want to have the library media specialist or principal listen and acknowledge the person's right to make his or her opinion known. The school library professional displays leadership qualities by respectfully listening to the complainant's concerns, whether they are voiced in person, over the telephone, or via email. Greeting the complainant with a smile and maintaining eye contact are two positive communication strategies. Another is being an "active listener" by acknowledging the person's complaint with a comment such as "I understand your concern" (ALA, Office for Intellectual Freedom, "Coping with Challenges; School Libraries; One-on-One"). During the conversation, explain that while parents may guide or restrict their own children's library selections, they must allow other parents the same right. In some cases, an informal discussion between the library professional and the complainant resolves the objections, and the matter ends with that conversation.

If the complainant is not satisfied and insists the item be removed from the library's collection, explain the reconsideration process and provide the necessary reconsideration form. It is very important to stress that no action is taken by school personnel unless a written, signed reconsideration form is returned. Some districts have a time period by which this action must be taken.

WHEN A CHALLENGE OCCURS

A library media specialist must always be ready for a challenge. It is impossible to know which resource may cause a parent, administrator, or faculty member to voice an oral complaint that may end in a formal, written request for reconsideration of the resource. The school library professional must know the immediate steps to take when an individual submits a written request for reconsideration of a library resource. Take these initial actions when a library resource is formally challenged:

- Review your institution's selection policy, including the selection criteria and the reconsideration process
- Assess what steps have been taken in the reconsideration process and what steps are to be taken
- Review the complaint
- Discuss the situation with your administrator
- Review your profession's policy statements
- Gather resources (such as copies of reviews, information on awards and best-of-the-year list distinctions for the title)
- Read or re-read the title in question (Cooperative Children's Book Center, "Suggested Steps")

Discussing the challenge with your principal, if he or she is not already aware of the complainant's concern, is essential. No administrator wants to be uninformed about possible problems. It is helpful to the principal if the school library media specialist prepares a one-page document including a short summary of the challenged resource, why it was selected, how it matches district selection policy criteria, quotations from reviews, a list of awards received, and a brief list of the steps included in the reconsideration process (Dickinson 2007, 22–23). The document provides the administrator with a welcome overview of the questioned item and establishes the school library professional as knowledgeable about collection resources. Also it is critical that the principal be knowledgeable about the reconsideration process and the steps that she or he must take to begin it. These may include forming a reconsideration committee to review the challenged resource or, ideally, contacting the standing reconsideration committee.

Some principals do not welcome the reconsideration process and wish to sidestep a challenge. If the principal appears unwilling to begin the process to review the questioned resource, there are several ways to give verbal or written cues about the need to follow district policy. The library media professional may suggest in person or in writing, "Maybe we can sit down and go over the reconsideration policy together, so we're each clear about the steps we need to take" (Cooperative Children's Book Center, "What IF?"). Another option is, "I know we both want to make sure the board-approved policy and procedures are followed at all times. If the book is removed at this point, it will be in violation of the board-approved policy" (Cooperative Children's Book Center, "What IF?").

If the principal asks the school library professional to remove the item from the collection temporarily or permanently, the American Library Association recommends, "Remind school administrators that to ignore or override a board-approved materials selection policy can place them in legal jeopardy" (ALA, Office for Intellectual Freedom, "Coping with Challenges; School Libraries; Preparing for Challenges"). It takes courage to ask a principal to follow policy, but consider the alternative. If a book or other library resource is removed outside the district's official process, where will this type of censorship end? In reality, the principal is asking an employee to circumvent district policy, and this action can have serious consequences for the individual.

What if a principal will not follow board-approved reconsideration procedures despite diplomatic efforts? A leader will try to clarify exactly what he or she is being asked to do by the principal with possible statements such as "Are you instructing me to disregard the official, board-approved policy of our district? Are you telling me to remove a book from the library without going through the district's procedures for reconsideration?" (Cooperative Children's Book Center, "What IF?"). The seriousness of these questions may shock the administrator into rethinking his or her reluctance to follow policy. If the answer remains to remove the item from the collection, the choices are to follow your principal's direct order or not to do so. Both actions have consequences and must be considered carefully.

To protect yourself when taking either action, keep copies of any written exchanges between you and the principal. If all discourse was verbal, make careful notes with dates and file them off school premises. If there is a teacher's union in the district, report the situation to an association official (Cooperative Children's Book Center, "What IF?"). If there is a district library media director, this matter should be shared with that individual. Lastly, this situation is a blend of employment law, district policy, and professional ethics. Call the American Library Association's Office for Intellectual Freedom staff for additional advice (800-545-2433, extension 4220).

OTHER RESPONSIBILITIES DURING A CHALLENGE

After ensuring that the principal understands and will support the reconsideration process, the school library professional will have other responsibilities. These include working with the reconsideration committee, soliciting support for retention of the library resource, possibly responding to media queries under district guidelines, and completing the final tasks when the reconsideration process concludes.

The Reconsideration Committee

When the reconsideration committee has been named or the standing committee alerted, the library media specialist will provide the committee with copies of the questioned resource, copies of reviews, and a list of awards, if any. She or he may also prepare a written analysis describing how the item meets the district's official selection criteria and serve as a resource to the committee during its deliberation.

The school library professional should be proactive in explaining minors' First Amendment rights to receive information and how the courts have viewed this right in notable First Amendment court cases such as *Board of Education, Island Trees Union Free School District No. 26, et al. v. Pico*, 457 U.S. 853 (1982) and the *Right to Read Defense Committee of Chelsea v. School Committee of the City of Chelsea*,

454 F. Supp. 703 (D. Mass. 1978). The media specialist can also advise the committee's chair and the principal on strategies to achieve a well-run public reconsideration hearing using suggestions found at the American Library Association's Office for Intellectual Freedom Web site.

Soliciting Support for Retention of the Library Resource

A school library media specialist need not and *should not* face a challenge alone. When a formal written challenge occurs, the library media specialist should seek support locally by contacting other school library professionals in the district. Adding to collegial support, the relationships and local personal network of allies that the school library media specialist has created through outreach efforts can be helpful. The library media specialist can ask teachers, students, parents, and community members who support the First Amendment rights of minors to write letters to the editor of the local newspaper and attend the public reconsideration hearing to support retaining the challenged resource in the collection with no restrictions. The school library professional can also seek guidance from the American Library Association's Office for Intellectual Freedom. It maintains a challenge support service and will provide assistance with potential and actual challenges to books, magazines, Internet access, and other library resources (ALA, Office for Intellectual Freedom, "Reporting a Challenge"). Staff at the Office for Intellectual Freedom can be reached at 800-545-2433, extension 4223.

The school library media specialist has a lengthy list of policy statements from the American Library Association on which to draw during a challenge. Carefully drafted by the Intellectual Freedom Committee with input from leaders within the organization and approved by the Council of the American Library Association, these statements are the "right words for the right time" and can be used to educate, advocate, and defend. The documents include the Library Bill of Rights and its many interpretations. They are available on the American Library Association's Web site (http://www.ala.org/ala/aboutala/offices/oif/statementspols/statementspolicies.cfm/).

Managing Media Coverage

Many school districts have a single individual designated as the media contact, and this staff person speaks officially for the district. The media can be a friend or a foe during a challenge, and leaders learn techniques to work with local newspapers and broadcast media effectively. If the district allows the library media specialist to comment on the challenge, one of the best sources for media tips is the American Library Association Web site. A few of their strategies include:

- Prepare carefully for any contacts with the media. Know the most important message you want to deliver and be able to deliver it in 25 words or less.
- Practice answering difficult questions and answers out loud.
- Keep it simple. Avoid professional jargon. Try to talk in user-friendly terms your audience can relate to: Freedom of choice—not the *Library Bill of Rights*. "People with concerns" or "concerned parents"—not censors.
- Remember, nothing is "off the record." Assume that anything you say could end up on the front page or leading the news broadcast. (ALA, Office for Intellectual Freedom, "Coping with Challenges, Dealing with the Media, More Tips")

When the Challenge Is Over

When the challenge has been resolved, a library media specialist displays leadership by working with the reconsideration committee and the principal to analyze the effectiveness of the reconsideration process during the recent challenge. If there are weaknesses in the policy and insufficient detail in the process, the policy should be revised, depending on whether the time is right politically. The school library professional should also report the challenge and its result to the American Library Association's Office for Intellectual Freedom using its online form. All information submitted is kept confidential and is used to determine the status of intellectual freedom in the United States. Statistics are also used to determine the American Library Association's annual list of "Most Frequently Challenged Books."

OTHER BARRIERS TO ACCESS

In addition to the possible removal of resources through challenges, there are other barriers to access to materials in a school library media center. School library professionals who are leaders speak out against barriers such as age or grade level restrictions that limit the number of books elementary students can check out, keep kindergarten students from checking out books for much of their first year in school, or restrict students to selecting a book only in their reading level. The school library media specialist also is dedicated to changing school policy that prohibits students with overdue books, fines, or unpaid lost resource fees from checking out materials. Fixed library schedules in elementary schools affect access to reading and research opportunities for young students. Inadequate budgets have an impact on the ability of the library media professional to purchase new and replacement resources, thereby affecting the usefulness of the collection for students. Finally, the elimination of school library professionals results in a leadership vacuum affecting students' information literacy and access to information. The total effect of all of these barriers to access is monumental, especially for those children or young adults for whom the school library is the *only* library they can use regularly. Lack of access to resources and the services of a credentialed library media specialist severely diminish students' intellectual freedom and their First Amendment right to read and receive information.

INTELLECTUAL FREEDOM ONLINE

At one time, librarians associated intellectual freedom solely with print and nonprint materials located on the shelves of a library; however, the Internet permits access to information never dreamed possible when school library collections were confined to what was available locally or via interlibrary loan. Despite the Internet's promise of limitless resources, students, teachers, and library media specialists in many schools are frustrated daily when they find legitimate educational Web sites blocked by their schools' filters. The filters are the result of the Children's Internet Protection Act, which requires schools and libraries that receive specified federal funds to use filters to block visual depictions of child pornography, obscenity, and material "harmful to minors" (Children's Internet Protection Act of 2000). It should be noted that in addition to the Children's Internet Protection Act, many states have legislation that requires filtering of Internet content in schools and/or libraries. Information on specific state filtering legislation is available at http://www.ncsl.org/programs/lis/cip/filterlaws.htm/.

Unfortunately, many districts block sites far beyond the requirements of the Children's Internet Protection Act in an effort to "protect" their students from unsavory content on the Web. Relying solely on filters to keep students safe does not teach students how to be savvy searchers or how to evaluate the accuracy of information. Christopher Harris said, "Filter a website, and you protect a student for a day. Educate students about online safety in the real world environment, and you protect your child for a lifetime" (Adams 2008, 141).

The principles of intellectual freedom should apply regardless of the format or method of delivery of the information. Filtering educational Web sites negatively affects students' ability to seek information to complete assignments and research personal interests. The American Library Association speaks to this access issue when it states,

Children and young adults unquestionably possess First Amendment rights, including the right to receive information through the library in print, nonprint, or digital format. Constitutionally protected speech cannot be suppressed solely to protect children or young adults from ideas or images a legislative body believes to be unsuitable for them. (ALA, "Free Access")

BUILDING SUPPORT FOR LESS RESTRICTIVE FILTERING

Since it unlikely that the Children's Internet Protection Act will be repealed or changed substantially in the near future, living with a filtering system is a fact of life in K–12 schools. This does not mean, however, that the school library professional should accept that students and faculty are blocked from accessing worthwhile online educational resources. To protect students' right to access legal online information in schools, the school library media specialist should provide the principal with specific examples of blocked educational Web resources experienced by teachers and students in the school. If the principal is supportive, request that administrators assemble a group representing all stakeholders—principals, teachers, technology staff, library media personnel, and parents—and discuss openly how the school community can use online resources to best support the learning of students while fulfilling its legal responsibility.

The group will have an opportunity to discuss what the law really requires and to determine how federal and possibly state filtering mandates will be implemented in the school district. While seated together, participants will hear the perspectives of teachers who have useful sites blocked, administrators who are responsible for protecting students in school, technology staff who manage the filters, library media specialists who advocate for minors' First Amendment right to access legal content online, and parents who entrust their children's safety and education to school staff. The experience will give those present a better understanding of the frustrations and challenges faced by all parties. Through examining the varying points of view represented, it will likely be possible to establish common ground on which to build policies and practices that adhere to the law but do not compromise access to educational resources. Within the discussion, encourage administrators and technology staff to set filters at the least restrictive position. Additionally, work toward creating an effective decision making process under which teachers and library staff may request erroneously blocked Web sites be unblocked *on a timely basis* for use in classroom and library research. The group should also determine criteria for staff requests to override the filter.

In 2008, Congress passed the Protecting Children in the 21st Century Act as part of the Broadband Data Services Improvement Act, and it was signed into law in October. The law requires K–12 schools receiving discounted services under the federal Schools and Libraries Program of the Universal Service Fund (the E-rate Program) to include within its Internet safety policy the educating of minors "about appropriate online behavior, including interacting with other individuals on social networking websites and in chat rooms and cyber bullying awareness and response" (Broadband Data Services Improvement Act of 2008). This legal requirement is the perfect opportunity for the library media specialist, as part of the assembled group, to urge the adoption of a comprehensive curriculum as a means of teaching students to use the Internet safely and ethically both in school and elsewhere. The group's discussion should also include the use of Web 2.0 interactive tools such as blogs, podcasts, wikis, and other emerging technologies.

The American Library Association recently approved "Minors and Internet Interactivity: An Interpretation of the Library Bill of Rights," which states:

The First Amendment applies to speech created by minors on interactive sites. Usage of these social networking sites in a school or library allows minors to access and create resources that fulfill their interests and needs for information, for social connection with peers, and for participation in a community of learners. Restricting expression and access to interactive Web sites because the sites provide tools for sharing information with others violates the tenets of the *Library Bill of Rights*. It is the responsibility of librarians and educators to monitor threats to the intellectual freedom of minors and to advocate for extending access to interactive applications on the Internet.

As defenders of intellectual freedom and the First Amendment, libraries and librarians have a responsibility to offer unrestricted access to Internet interactivity in accordance with local, state, and federal laws and to advocate for greater access where it is abridged. School and library professionals should work closely with young people to help them learn skills and attitudes that will prepare them to be responsible, effective, and productive communicators in a free society. (ALA 2009)

The leadership shown by the school library media specialist during the group's discussions of access to and use of online resources and during subsequent implementation of policies and plans will help preserve students' intellectual freedom online.

PRIVACY

It is the responsibility of library media specialists to protect the privacy of students using resources and services in their library media centers and to maintain the confidentiality of students' library records. There are two sources of support for student privacy. The first is state and federal laws, and the second is policy statements from the American Library Association and the American Association of School Librarians.

Nearly every state has laws that protect the confidentiality of school library records. Since these laws vary greatly, a school library professional needs to be knowledgeable about his or her state's library records law and be able to interpret how it affects the confidentiality of student library records. It is important to note that at this time, state library records laws, or opinions from attorneys general, protect the confidentiality of school library media center records in all states except Florida, Maine, Connecticut, and Massachusetts. State library records laws are archived on the American Library Association's Web site (http://www.ala.org/ala/aboutala/offices/oif/ifgroups/stateifcchairs/ stateifcinaction/stateprivacy.cfm).

At the federal level, the Family Educational Rights and Privacy Act (FERPA) protects the confidentiality of K–12 and post-secondary students' "education records." FERPA guidance lists many types of records to be kept confidential, but it does not list library records. Although the Family Policy Compliance Office has not issued *written* guidance on this matter, according to Ingrid Brault, an employee in that office,

Under FERPA, "education records" are defined as those records that are directly related to a student and maintained by an educational agency or institution or by a party acting for the agency or institution. 34 CFR § 99.3 "Education records." As such, we advise schools that library circulation records as you describe them [records of books and other materials checked out by students with the student's name attached to the record of each item s/he has checked out] meet the definition of education records under FERPA and cannot generally be disclosed absent consent of the parent unless an exception to the consent requirement applies. (Brault email)

Brault delineated those exceptions when education records, including library records, can be disclosed without parental consent as being:

- to *appropriately designated school officials with legitimate educational interest*, [34 CFR § 99.31 (a)(1) School Officials] [emphasis added], or
- if all the conditions apply under FERPA's health and safety provisions [34 CFR § 99.36] . . . , or
- if any of the exceptions listed under section 99.31 of the FERPA regulations applies such as in compliance with a lawfully issued court order or subpoena. (Brault email)

Although there are exceptions within FERPA that allow the disclosure of a student's education record without parental approval, the American Library Association Office for Intellectual Freedom has provided some clarification with respect to FERPA requirements.

FERPA . . . *permits* disclosure of school library records when state library confidentiality statutes and professional ethics would otherwise prohibit such disclosure. FERPA, however, *does not require* the institution to disclose records under these circumstances nor does FERPA require institutions to create or maintain particular records. (Scales 2009, 75)

The American Library Association's Office for Intellectual Freedom counsels schools and libraries to undertake the following actions to protect student library records:

- craft policies that extend additional privacy protection to students' library records;
- adopt record retention policies that protect students' confidentiality in regard to their use of the library media center; and,
- where applicable, incorporate state law protections for library records. (Scales 2009, 75)

Beyond state and federal laws, the American Library Association and the American Association of School Librarians have policy statements related to protecting minors'

School Library Media Program Privacy Checklist

I have . . .	Met	Not Yet or District Level Decision	Next Steps
* Educated myself about state and federal laws affecting minors' privacy in schools and libraries and reviewed American Library Association policy statements related to privacy and personally identifiable information (PII) about patrons.			
* Analyzed my state's library records law and understand how it applies to student library records.			
* Inquired how the Family Educational Rights and Privacy Act (FERPA) applies to local school library records.			
*Developed a privacy policy stating what PII is collected, who may access library patron records, and the circumstances under which minors' records may be released legally; incorporated state library record law protections where applicable; extended the maximum privacy protections possible, and sought formal approval of the policy by the school board or institution's governing body.			
* Posted the library's privacy policy for patrons to read.			
* Supported library procedures granting the maximum privacy possible to students regardless of age.			
* Protected circulation records with passwords and provided different levels of access for students, volunteers, and library staff.			
* Configured automation software to delete students' circulation history.			
* Created a records retention policy that protects students' privacy by retaining library user records for the shortest period possible and destroying records when they are no longer needed.			
* Retained as few student library records as possible and purged library records identifying individual students' use of resources and services on a regular basis.			

Continued

I have . . .	Met	Not Yet or District Level Decision	Next Steps
* Trained library staff, volunteers, and student assistants about the confidentiality of all library records, instructing them not to examine circulation records of others.			
* Proactively educated administrators and teachers about the confidentiality of student library records.			
* Taught students to respect the confidentiality of library records—their own and those of others.			
* Informed students of overdue materials in a manner that respects their privacy.			
* Protected students' interlibrary loan and reserve requests from the scrutiny of non-library staff.			
* Modeled best practice by making sure that conversations with students about materials being checked out or used in the library media center are confidential.			
* Guarded information gained through student use of resources and services by not divulging it indiscriminately to faculty, administrators, or others.			
* Refrained from affixing labels denoting a book's reading level or leveling a collection to avoid having students learn the reading levels of their peers.			
* Supported incorporating privacy into the district's acceptable use policy (AUP).			
* Included information about protecting one's privacy online as part of instruction on Internet safety.			
* Encouraged students to realize that citizens have privacy rights under the 4th and 5th Amendments, state, and federal laws.			
* Reached out to parents by communicating library policy as it relates to student privacy and providing information about protecting minors' privacy online.			

I have ...	Met	Not Yet or District Level Decision	Next Steps
* Demonstrated personal judgment when violating a student's privacy by speaking to a counselor or principal out of concern for a student's welfare.			
* Counseled that surveillance camera(s) not be aimed at the circulation desk or be intrusive in recording actions of persons using the school library media center.			
* Discussed privacy concerns with vendors of any technology currently owned or under consideration for purchase and requested that they include privacy protections in future software changes.			

Reprinted with permission by Libraries Unlimited from the original checklist published in *School Library Media Activities Monthly* 25 (5) (March 2009): 55.

privacy rights in libraries. The *Code of Ethics of the American Library Association* states in Article III, "We protect each library user's right to privacy and confidentiality with respect to information sought or received and resources consulted, borrowed, acquired, or transmitted" (ALA 2007). The American Association of School Librarians' "Position Statement on the Confidentiality of Library Records" declares, "The library community recognizes that children and youth have the same rights to privacy as adults" (American Association of School Librarians, "Position Statement"). Finally, the American Library Association's "Privacy: An Interpretation of the Library Bill of Rights" reminds school library professionals of their obligation "to an ethic of facilitating, not monitoring access to information" (ALA, Office for Intellectual Freedom, "Privacy"). Where legal protections do not apply to school library records, these documents provide a strong ethical defense for school library professionals defending minors' privacy when using a school library media center.

Every day in school library media centers, situations occur in which students' privacy is either protected or disregarded. For example, when notifying students of overdue library materials, does the school library media specialist print notices that include the names of the students and the titles of the overdue items and give them to a teacher to distribute? Or does the media specialist protect each student's privacy by folding and stapling the notification and leaving only the student's name visible, not the titles of late, unreturned materials. In another example, if a teacher asks whether a student has checked out a specific title, does the school library professional answer the question or state that student library records are confidential? The difference between the outcomes of the two examples depends on whether the school library media specialist correctly interprets state and/or federal laws, accepts privacy as one of the core values of librarianship, and has the moral courage to act on those principles. For additional information on protecting the privacy of students using the school library media center, consult Chapter 5, "Privacy in the School Media Program," in *Ensuring Intellectual*

Freedom and Access to Information in the School Library Media Program, by Helen R. Adams (Libraries Unlimited, 2008).

There are a wide range of actions school library professionals can take to protect the privacy of students in the school media center. Use the "School Library Media Program Privacy Checklist" to determine the status of student privacy in your facility.

Because of the protective nature of American adults toward children, the right of privacy for minors is not easy to defend; however, library media specialists have the most knowledge of library records law and intellectual freedom concepts and bear the greatest responsibility to protect the privacy of their student patrons. Students will only feel comfortable to research topics and make personal reading choices if they are confident that their use of library resources will be kept confidential by library staff.

ADVOCACY @ YOUR SCHOOL LIBRARY

Leaders are proactive rather than reactive. They plan ahead and strategize the steps needed to achieve their program and personal goals. They maintain open communication with the administration and all staff in the school. To be an effective advocate, a school library media specialist must be knowledgeable about current intellectual freedom issues at the local, state, and national levels. He or she must read professional literature; review the American Library Association's Office for Intellectual Freedom Web site and blog frequently; subscribe to listservs such as LM_Net, where intellectual freedom issues are discussed; sign up for the American Library Association's IFAction electronic news-only list, which disseminates media reports on intellectual freedom issues; and attend relevant conferences, workshops, and webinars. Advocating for intellectual freedom is a continuous process that requires outreach and collaboration with those who can be the school library professionals' best allies—administrators, teachers, students, parents, and the larger community outside the school.

Advocacy with Principals

Principals set the tone and direction for their schools. Former school administrator Gary Hartzell stated in his presentation at the 2002 White House Conference on School Libraries, "The principal is a key player, perhaps *the* key player [emphasis added], in library media programs that make a difference" (Church 2009, 40). Since administrators do not receive training about intellectual freedom in their coursework, it is the responsibility of the library media specialist to help the principal understand students' right to access information in the school library. Use these strategies to inform a principal about intellectual freedom and why it is important in every school.

- Connect students' free access to legal information in the school library media center collection to the education of "future" citizens.
- Meet with the principal to review the materials selection policy and procedures for acquisition. Follow-up activities could include sending the principal lists of new materials and inviting him/her to the media center to view new resource displays.
- Review the district's reconsideration procedures annually with the principal. Clarify any steps or responsibilities in the reconsideration process that are in question.

- Gain the respect of the principal by providing a brief written memo and initiate oral discussion on an aspect of intellectual freedom as issues arise.
- Avoid library jargon, and include examples to make the concepts of intellectual freedom more concrete. (Adams 2008, 204–205)

The principal can be a valuable ally supporting the library media program's goal of protecting students' access to information in all formats, maintaining the confidentiality of their library records, and providing resources reflecting a broad range of ideas. An uneducated principal can also be a hindrance, thwarting the efforts of the library media professional to protect minors' First Amendment and other legal rights. In most cases, the difference between a school climate that is "intellectual freedom friendly" and one where the principal and library media specialist are at odds is the *knowledge of the principal*. An administrator who is informed and nurtured about how intellectual freedom principles are applied in the day-to-day educating of students and their library use will become a partner and support the leadership efforts of the school library professional.

Teaching Teachers about Intellectual Freedom

Teacher education courses also do not include information on intellectual freedom, students' First Amendment right to access information in the school library, or state library record laws. Similar to the principal, teachers can be valuable allies. It is essential to cultivate and develop relationships with staff over time to help them understand the purposes of the school library program and its effect on students' curricular and personal growth. Be the "visible" library media specialist instructing teachers about intellectual freedom by using these strategies:

- Meet with new teaching staff prior to the beginning of the school year to explain library policies related to materials selection, reconsideration of a challenged resource, privacy of library records, interlibrary loan, and Internet use.
- Review the reconsideration process and its various steps with veteran staff annually since a teacher may be the first person to hear a parent complaint about a library resource.
- Request faculty meeting or staff development time to explain the library's materials selection policy, selection criteria, and the need for collection diversity. Invite teachers to recommend titles or subject areas for purchase.
- Plan collaboratively with teachers to provide students with learning experiences incorporating First Amendment speech rights, privacy, evaluation of information, and safe and effective online searching (Adams 2008, 206).

The American Association of School Librarians' *Empowering Learners: Guidelines for School Library Media Programs* emphasizes the changing role of the school library media specialist and ranks *instructional partner* as the number one role for the twenty-first-century school library professional. The Guidelines portray the school library media specialist as assisting teachers in developing learning objectives and goals and as a collaborator with teachers developing assignments that match academic standards (American Association of School Librarians 2009, 16–17). The media specialist assumes the role of instructional partner when she or he works with teachers to educate students about their legal rights and the negative results of censorship.

The time and effort spent in helping teachers understand the legal and ethical aspects of students' intellectual freedom can produce two benefits. First, teachers will be able to incorporate the information into their instruction as appropriate. Second, if a challenge occurs, because of their knowledge colleagues may oppose the censorship attempt to remove a resource from the school library collection or restrict access to it.

Educating Students about Intellectual Freedom

School library media specialists play a key role in teaching students about their First Amendment rights in school libraries and laws protecting the confidentiality of minors' library use—all integral aspects of their intellectual freedom. Standard 3 of the American Association of School Librarians' *Standards for the 21st-Century Learner* states, "Learners use skills, resources, & tools to: Share knowledge and participate ethically and productively as members of our democratic society." Also listed is corresponding Student Responsibility 3.37: "Respect the principles of intellectual freedom" (American Association of School Librarians 2007).

Students will not be able to understand and respect the principles of intellectual freedom and their legal rights in libraries unless they are taught about them. Students are "citizens in training," and the library media specialist builds a collection that provides them with many perspectives on the issues confronting citizens in a democratic society. Providing access to a wide range of materials is not sufficient, however. The school library professional must help students make the connection between free access to information and their responsibility as citizens to make informed decisions. School library professionals can inform students using these strategies:

- Appeal to students by using "kid friendly" language. Students may not be familiar with the term *intellectual freedom*, but they can likely identify with the concept of *access*. In this context, *access* means having a school library collection that provides them with information reflecting many points of view and in a variety of formats.
- Display intellectual freedom documents prominently in the library including the Bill of Rights of the U.S. Constitution [http://www.constitution.org/billofr_.htm], the Library Bill of Rights [http://www.ala.org/ala/aboutala/offices/oif/statementspols/statementsif/librarybillrights.cfm], and the Universal Declaration of Human Rights (especially Article 19) [http://www.un.org/Overview/rights.html]. Explain their connection to the library, and refer to them during information literacy skills instruction. Post news articles, cartoons, and posters to provide daily reminders of intellectual freedom and its importance in our society.
- Celebrate Banned Books Week in September. Attract students' attention by creating displays of books that have been challenged, providing information about the First Amendment and banned books via the school's public address system, giving away bookmarks promoting the freedom to read, presenting book talks on "banned" books, and encouraging teachers to incorporate the theme of banned books and censorship into their lessons.
- Encourage students to participate in selecting and recommending new materials. Use selection policy criteria such as "reflect the pluralistic nature of a global society" or "free of bias and stereotyping" to teach students about the right of all members of a democratic society, including minors, to view, listen to, and read materials with diverse perspectives.
- Turn ordinary library situations into teaching opportunities about privacy. For example, if a student is looking for a book not on the shelf and asks who has checked it out, library staff can explain that information about who has borrowed the item from the library is confidential,

referencing the library program's privacy policy and their state's library record law. (Adams 2009, 55)

Reaching Out to Families

Parents, guardians, and extended family members are interested in the education and success of their children and young adults. Every family's values are different. Some parents or guardians may support the library media program's efforts to offer students a collection on a wide range of topics from varied perspectives. Others may feel all minors, especially younger children, must be protected from library materials they view as incorporating offensive language, sexual explicitness, violence, positive portrayal of homosexuality, and religious or political points of view at odds with their own. Parents have the responsibility and right to guide their children's reading and information-seeking choices; however, those who challenge books or other library resources to "protect" all youth take away the right of other families to decide for themselves.

Like others outside the library profession, parents and community members may not be familiar with the term *intellectual freedom*; therefore, the best approach may be to speak about "choice" and how the school library provides a wide range of materials to support the curriculum and meet students' interests, taking into consideration their social development, emotional maturity, and reading levels. The school library media specialist shows leadership by proactively describing how library materials are selected. To support this effort, the board-approved materials selection policy should be posted on the library's Web site. New library materials can be highlighted through a school or library newsletter sent to families. It is equally important to explain the district's reconsideration process, rationale for the process, and the steps involved. The school library professional can become acquainted with parents and other family members through presentations about the changing library program, hosting a library open house, or soliciting library volunteers. Every contact should be considered as *an opportunity* to build a positive relationship and advocate for students' right to read and find information in the school library (Adams 2008, 213–215). The trust and respect built through the relationships may over time develop into support for the program during a challenge, district financial crisis, or library staff reductions.

CONCLUSION

Intellectual freedom is one of the core values of librarianship, and this chapter has outlined the many responsibilities of school library media specialists to increase and preserve intellectual freedom in school library media programs. School library professionals provide leadership and advocate for intellectual freedom when they:

- Maintain a high level of personal knowledge about current intellectual freedom issues at the local, state, and national levels
- Encourage the creation and regular review of a board-approved materials selection policy
- Select library resources without succumbing to self-censorship
- Build positive relationships with teaching colleagues, administrators, students, and parents through participation in professional and student-centered activities
- Prepare for a future challenge to a library resource by developing supporters of minors' First Amendment rights among administrators, teachers, parents, and other community members

- Treat those with concerns about library resources respectfully and acknowledge their right to voice personal opinions
- Work with the principal to ensure that the reconsideration process is followed
- Provide members of the reconsideration committee with the information needed to complete the review process
- Solicit support for retaining a challenged library resource
- Seek to eliminate economic and other barriers to access to school library media program resources
- Provide rationale for why students' access to quality Internet educational resources and interactive Web technologies should be increased
- Protect the privacy of students using library resources and services and maintain the confidentiality of students' library records
- Establish strategies for informing the principal and teachers about students' First Amendment rights
- Teach students about their intellectual freedom and First Amendment right to access information in the school library media center
- Reach out to parents and the community to explain how materials are selected and the need for a collection with diverse points of view

The responsibilities related to intellectual freedom are integral to being a school library media specialist, and leaders keep them in the forefront of their daily work. By taking a leadership role in promoting students' intellectual freedom, school library media specialists are able to encourage sustained positive change.

BASIC INTELLECTUAL FREEDOM RESOURCES

- Adams, Helen R. *Ensuring Intellectual Freedom and Access to Information in the School Library Media Program*. Westport, CT: Libraries Unlimited, 2008.
- American Library Association, Office for Intellectual Freedom. http://www.ala.org/oif.
- Cooperative Children's Book Center, School of Education, University of Wisconsin–Madison. "What IF? Questions and Answers on Intellectual Freedom." http://www.education.wisc.edu/ccbc/freedom/whatif/default.asp.
- Scales, Pat. *Protecting Intellectual Freedom in Your School Library*. Chicago: American Library Association, 2009.

REFERENCES

Adams, Helen R. 2008. *Ensuring intellectual freedom and access to information in the school library media program*. Westport, CT: Libraries Unlimited.

———. 2009. IF matters: Intellectual freedom @ your library, citizens in training: Twelve ways to teach students about intellectual freedom. *School Library Media Activities Monthly* 25 (8): 55.

American Association of School Librarians. 2007. *Standards for the 21st-century learner*. http://www.ala.org/ala/mgrps/divs/aasl/guidelinesandstandards/learningstandards/standards.cfm (accessed May 5, 2009).

———. 2009. *Empowering learners: Guidelines for school library media programs*. Chicago: American Association of School Librarians.

———. Position statement on the confidentiality of library records. http://www.ala.org/ala/mgrps/divs/aasl/aaslproftools/positionstatements/aaslpositionstatementconfidentiality.cfm (accessed April 20, 2009).

American Library Association (ALA). 2007. *Code of ethics of the American Library Association.* http://www.ala.org/ala/aboutala/offices/oif/statementspols/codeofethics/codeethics.cfm (accessed April 20, 2009).

———. 2009. ALA Intellectual Freedom Committee report to Council, 2009 annual conference, Chicago, IL, Wednesday July 15, 2009.http://www.ala.org/ala/aboutala/offices/oif/ifgroups/ifcommittee/intellectual.cfm (accessed July 21, 2009).

———. Core values of librarianship. http://www.ala.org/ala/aboutala/offices/oif/statementspols/corevaluesstatement/corevalues.cfm#service (accessed March 5, 2009).

———. Free Access to Libraries by Minors: An Interpretation of the Library Bill of Rights. http://www.ala.org/ala/aboutala/offices/oif/statementspols/statementsif/interpretations/freeaccesslibraries.cfm/http://www.ala.org/ala/aboutala/offices/oif/statementspols/statementsif/interpretations/freeaccesslibraries.cfm/ (accessed April 20, 2009).

American Library Association (ALA), Office for Intellectual Freedom. Coping with challenges; school libraries; one-on-one.http://www.ala.org/ala/aboutala/offices/oif/challengesupport/dealing/copingchallengesstrategies.cfm#protecting (accessed March 20, 2009).

———. Coping with challenges; school libraries; preparing for challenges. http://www.ala .org/ala/aboutala/offices/oif/challengesupport/dealing/copingchallengesstrategies.cfm #protecting (accessed March 19, 2009).

———. Privacy: An interpretation of the Library Bill of Rights. http://www.ala.org/ala/aboutala/offices/oif/statementspols/statementsif/interpretations/privacy.cfm/ (accessed February 8, 2010).

———. Reporting a challenge. http://www.ala.org/ala/issuesadvocacy/banned/challengeslibrary materials/challengereporting/index.cfm.

———. Strategies and Tips for Dealing with Challenges to Library Materials. http://www.ala.org/ala/issuesadvocacy/banned/challengeslibrarymaterials/copingwithchallenges/strategiestips/index.cfm#media (accessed March 10, 2010).

Brault, Ingrid, for the Family Policy Compliance Office. Email to the author. August 11, 2009.

Broadband Data Services Improvement Act of 2008, PL110-385. Title II. Protecting children, Section 215, Promoting online safety in schools. http://frwebgate.access.gpo.gov/cgi-bin/getdoc.cgi ?dbname=110_cong_public_laws&docid=f:publ385.110.pdf (accessed April 28, 2009).

Children's Internet Protection Act of 2000, PL 106-554. http://www.cdt.org/legislation/106th/speech/001218cipa.pdf/.

Church, Audrey P. 2009. The principal factor. *Library Media Connection* 27 (6): 40.

Cooperative Children's Book Center. Suggested steps to take when materials are challenged. http://www.education.wisc.edu/ccbc/freedom/steps.asp (accessed March 18, 2009).

———. What IF? question 52. http://www.education.wisc.edu/ccbc/freedom/whatif/archiveDetails.asp?idIFQuestions=52 (accessed March 19, 2009).

Dickinson, Gail. 2007. The challenges of a challenge: What to do? part II. *School Library Media Activities Monthly* 23 (6): 22–23.

Scales, Pat R., for the Office for Intellectual Freedom. 2009. *Protecting intellectual freedom in your school library: Scenarios from the front lines.* Chicago: American Library Association.

Ward, Susan. Leadership. About.com: Small Business: Canada. http://sbinfocanada.about.com/od/leadership/g/leadership.htm (accessed February 19, 2009).

Whelan, Debra Lau. 2009. A dirty little secret: Self-censorship. *School Library Journal* (February 1). http://www.schoollibraryjournal.com/article/CA6632974.html&/ (accessed March 5, 2009).

Wolf, Sara. 2008. Coping with mandated restrictions on intellectual freedom in K–12 schools. *Library Media Connection* 27 (3): 10–11.

5

Literacy Leadership and the School Library

Doug Achterman

In some respects, the school librarian's role as a literacy leader has not changed for generations. In 1931, Lucile Fargo noted that one aim of the school librarian is "to put excellent cultural, vocational, scientific, and recreational reading facilities within the grasp of every child of school age, and to stimulate the reading habit as an important item in mental health and intellectual progress and as a significant part in the training of youth in the proper use of leisure" (236). Literacy is a cornerstone of lifelong learning and at the core of a school library program's mission. Literacy leadership is still very much about doing all the things within the school librarian's range of influence to help students read, read more, read better, and read for a lifetime.

Much of literacy leadership is rooted in the values promoted through school librarianship's standards. Indeed, the first of the "common beliefs" described in the American Association of School Librarians' *Standards for the 21st-Century Learner* (2007) is that "reading is a window to the world":

Reading is a foundational skill for learning, personal growth, and enjoyment. The degree to which students can read and understand text in all formats (e.g., picture, video, print) and all contexts is a key indicator of success in school and in life. As a lifelong learning skill, reading goes beyond decoding and comprehension to interpretation and development of new understandings. (2)

But our understanding of literacy—and therefore literacy leadership—has evolved in the digital age. Technology has become a powerful tool in service to the school librarian's literacy goals, not only in promoting reading, but in assessing and improving students' skills. More significantly, though, technology has actually expanded the definition of literacy.

This chapter explores literacy leadership in the digital age, looking at a broad spectrum of issues a school librarian might consider when advancing the library program's literacy goals, as well as at ways technology both serves and changes our notions of literacy. These issues include the following:

- Creating and communicating a vision for literacy
- Modeling and promoting a love of reading
- Remembering Ranganathan: collecting for your population and creating a system that works for students and staff
- Working with the school site and district to create complementary goals
- Becoming a literacy expert and sharing knowledge with staff
- Collaborating with teachers to plan, teach, and evaluate lessons that promote literacy
- Deepening our understanding of how literacy is changing

The discussion of literacy leadership in this chapter is extensive but by no means exhaustive. In my own practice as a high school librarian, the time I have devoted to each facet of this role has been uneven. Any school librarian able to simultaneously exert leadership in each area discussed would be superhuman, especially considering the many other demands of the job beyond a focus on literacy. What is important, though, is sustained attention to each facet and an awareness of which areas will result in the most positive benefit for your students and school community.

PART I: CREATING AND COMMUNICATING A VISION FOR LITERACY

The school library is part of a larger educational system that usually includes at least the school site and the school district, both of which have discrete educational goals driven by a mission and a vision. As a literacy leader, the school librarian needs to develop a vision of literacy that both aligns with the goals of the broader school community and pushes that community forward.

In *Literacy Leadership: Six Strategies for Peoplework*, Donald McAndrew (2005) recommends beginning with the creation of a personal vision of literacy, offering practical activities to elicit that vision. McAndrew suggests reflecting on the role of literacy in one's own life through the creation of a personal literacy "lifeline," finding or creating a visual representation of the vision, writing a magazine article about one's future self as a literacy leader, and listing projected accomplishments in that vision. These reflections are followed by a one-page personal statement of the vision and the creation of a slogan that evokes the vision (e.g., "Spartans are readers!" or "Read, write, learn"). In the formation of that vision, McAndrew also recommends ongoing communication with all stakeholders—students, teachers, administrators, school board members, and other school community members—and incorporating their good ideas into the vision. These activities are designed to help school leaders consider literacy goals from a variety of angles and to think deeply about the ideal literacy future for the teacher leader (or librarian), for students, for the school community, and for the broader profession.

The thoughtful creation of a literacy vision helps set priorities and informs the day-to-day decisions of the school librarian. Frequent communication of that vision to others helps the school community maintain literacy as a primary focus of its own larger vision. Simply seeing the school librarian should prompt questions such as

- What am I doing to become a better reader and writer?
- How can I add a piece to my lesson that deepens or expands the reading or writing experience?
- What will this policy or decision do to help our literacy goals?
- What am I doing to promote literacy?

When the school librarian speaks as part of a faculty meeting or as a member of a school committee, others should anticipate questions that reflect a deep commitment to a vision of literacy for the entire school community. A literacy orientation should emanate from the school librarian, so that ultimately others in the school community assume some of that orientation themselves in their decisions and actions.

How often should this vision be revisited? Whenever it stops working. Without a picture in your head about what you want your students, teachers, and school community to become, you may fill your days with work but see little accomplished in this area. Much of the rest of this chapter discusses ideas and actions for literacy leadership that may arise out of such a vision.

PART II: MODELING AND PROMOTING A LOVE OF READING

For most librarians, modeling a love of reading is second nature. Michael Cart, author, *Booklist* reviewer, former library director, past president of the Young Adult Library Services Association, and a tireless promoter of young adult literature and reading, says, "As a reading and youth advocate, I always have a book with me because I believe that I can model reading behavior for anyone who happens to see me" (2007, 8–9). But, continues Cart, it is not enough just to be seen reading. School librarians "must be seen enjoying reading" and share their reading experiences with others "enthusiastically, even passionately" (2007, 9).

A tried-and-true outlet for that enthusiasm is the booktalk. A booktalk is essentially a performance designed to entice an audience to read a book. There is no single right way to do a booktalk, but among the many authors who have written on the subject, some common advice emerges:

- Know your audience.
- Grab students' attention right away.
- Share an incident or episode that represents the story without giving anything away.
- Write out or at least outline each booktalk so you are organized and prepared.
- Practice, practice, practice!
- Keep it short.
- Read the books you booktalk.

There are dozens of great models for how to do booktalks well, including Web sites, books, and videos offering tips for presenting. A good starting point for novice book-talkers is Nancy Keane's Booktalks—Quick and Simple Web site (http://nancykeane.com/booktalks/). Keane provides nearly 1,000 booktalks for students of all ages, retrievable by author, subject, title, and interest level. A "Booktalking Tips" page culls suggestions from LM_Net, a school librarians' listserv; Keane has added both teacher- and student-created booktalks, as well as daily booktalk podcasts. Joni Bodart has written over a dozen booktalking books, including several featuring her own booktalks of children's and young adults' award winners. Her *Booktalk! 2: Booktalking for All Ages and Audiences* (1985) provides lots of practical advice for booktalking in a school setting.

Booktalks are a way for school librarians to show they both know and love to read books of all kinds and for all audiences. As literacy leaders, school librarians understand they are modeling not just for students but for teachers and staff as well. Often I have begun a staff development session at my own school with a 60-second booktalk, ending with a reminder that students, too, enjoy it when their teachers talk about what they are reading. Collaborating with a classroom teacher is another effective way to do booktalks; the interaction provides additional interest, and teachers buy in to the value of the activity. Ultimately, school librarians and teachers can work with students to do their own booktalks, closing the loop not only in reading but in sharing with others their enthusiasm for good books.

While there is an abundance of prepared booktalks available, booktalkers are advised to use these only as aids in preparing their own talks. The time spent reading titles and preparing original talks will translate to more convincing preparations; in addition, students know a poser when they see one.

The Web offers an abundance of resources and tools for booktalkers. In addition to Nancy Keane's site (http://nancykeane.com/booktalks/), the University of Central Florida has begun a database of video booktalks of popular tween and teen titles. Digital Booktalk (http://digitalbooktalk.com) was conceived as a means to help reluctant readers find motivation to read and to afford another way to connect to a text. Video trailers—a kind of booktalk—have been created by graduate students and, more recently, by adolescents under their teachers' supervision.

Naomi Bates, school librarian at Northwest High School in Justin, Texas, maintains YA Books and More (http://naomibates.blogspot.com/), a blog that offers both print reviews of new young adult titles and video trailers. These trailers include brief bits of text, punctuated by images and sounds that communicate the feel of a particular book—a decidedly multimedia approach to booktalks. Bates has created a guide for other school librarians wishing to create these high-interest videos (http://naomibates .blogspot.com/2008/07/how-i-create-digital-booktrailers.html).

For younger students, Book Wink (http://www.bookwink.com), hosted by Sonja Cole and Paul Kim, offers video podcasts of theme-based booktalks. Aiming at third-to eighth-grade audiences, Cole typically booktalks three books on a single theme; themes of past podcasts range from love and popularity to volcanoes and World War II.

Students at Springfield Township High School, where Joyce Valenza is the school librarian, have created video trailers to introduce other students to the summer reading titles (http://springfieldvideo.edublogs.org/taxonomy/tags/book-trailers/). Student videos are truly a testimony of literacy leadership: ultimately, it is the students themselves who demonstrate their love of reading and share their enthusiasm with others.

School librarians can further promote a love of reading through sponsoring, organizing, or encouraging book clubs for students, staff, and school community members. There are as many ways of organizing book clubs as there are clubs themselves. When considering how to set up a book club, remembering to foster a love of reading as a sort of prime directive is helpful. If overly academic discussions seem to be killing the club's joy, it is time to try a new approach. As most book clubs a school librarian will sponsor are for students, a student-centered structure may work best. The ReadWriteThink site from the National Council of Teachers of English (http://www.readwritethink.org/lessons/lesson_view.asp?id=67) offers a sensible guideline for setting up successful book clubs at the elementary level—one that is easily adaptable to higher grades.

At large schools where there is just one librarian, the Internet has become a valuable tool for creating and sustaining book clubs. Frances Jacobson Harris, librarian at University Laboratory High School in Urbana, Illinois, maintains a threaded discussion site for students to talk to each other about books (https://www.uni.uiuc.edu/bbs/viewforum.php?f=5). Organized by genre, the site allows readers to contribute in short bursts, generally not with in-depth reflections but more as a social opportunity to share enthusiasm for a book, author, or series. The most active of these is currently the fantasy thread, which brims with discussion about a recent novel's translation to the big screen.

School library book club blogs spring up almost daily. One advantage of online book clubs is that several can be managed at once. Book clubs can be formed around a single popular title, an author, a genre, or any other way that will build an audience. Beyond providing a forum for students to share their own love of books, such book clubs might also attract parents, teachers, and non-teaching staff, creating a true school community of readership.

Sites such as GoodReads (http://www.goodreads.com), LibraryThing (http://www.librarything.com/), Shelfari (http://www.shelfari.com), and Delicious Monster (http://www.delicious-monster.com) offer Web 2.0 opportunities to create online communities of book lovers who share reviews and recommendations with others.

In addition to book talks and book clubs, librarians promote literacy through programs and events, from million-word reading campaigns to author visits, from poetry slams and Halloween scary story sleepovers to national events like "Read Across America" and "Teen Read Week." Such activities provide opportunities for all members of the school community to experience how richly rewarding reading and writing can be. RoseMary Honnold's *101+ Teen Programs That Work* (2002) and *More Teen Programs That Work* (2005) offer successful programming ideas—many of which emphasize literacy—from libraries throughout the United States.

A final, simple, low-tech way to promote conversation about reading is to provide each staff member—teachers, administrators, non-teaching staff—with an illustrated page that says, "Right now I'm reading ____." Staff can use an overhead projector pen to write in their current choice, and the laminated sheet can be used over and over again. This easy entry into every classroom and office on campus creates surprising conversations among school community members who might otherwise never speak to one another. Real leadership in fostering and promoting a love of reading shows when others take up the cause as enthusiastically as does the school librarian.

PART III: REMEMBERING RANGANATHAN: COLLECTING FOR YOUR POPULATION AND CREATING A SYSTEM THAT WORKS FOR STUDENTS AND STAFF

Being a literacy leader also means setting in place policies and procedures that communicate a consistent message about the fundamental importance of literacy. Ranganathan's (1931) first two laws of library science, "Books are for use" and "Every reader his [or her] book," are helpful to consider when implementing such policies and procedures.

Books Are for Use

In a print context, Ranganathan's first law creates implications for both collection development and circulation policies. School libraries are typically wanting for physical space; books that do not support the curriculum or the school community's recreational reading interests should be removed from the collection. Limited new materials budgets should not discourage this practice. Why is this a leadership issue? Librarians do not view collections the same way others do. Many people look at shelves loaded with books and assume there are plenty of resources, which may justify a trimmed budget or maintenance of the status quo at best. If the collection is kept lean, so that the books which remain truly get used, suddenly the shelves may begin to look bare, and members of the school community will begin to see—literally—that the collection needs to be increased.

Circulation policies, furthermore, should be designed to maximize the use of resources. A multitude of studies indicate that students benefit from reading a wide variety of materials in a wide variety of formats (see Cipielewski and Stanovich 1992; Cunningham and Stanovich 1991; Guthrie and Schafer 2001; Krisch et al. 2002). Liberal circulation policies on quantity and type of books checked out benefit students and teachers and are a regular reminder that the library program supports and leads literacy efforts in the school community.

In a digital context, Ranganathan's first law suggests a collection that is streamlined and tailored to the interests and needs of a particular school population. Ideally, a school library's digital collection offers 24/7 access to both subscription and free Web content for students and teachers. The organization of that material should be easily grasped by the student population with a minimum of instruction. Subscription access should be as simple as possible; content that requires students to set up individual registrations, log-ins, and ID numbers only discourages use and serves to undermine the literacy leadership status of the librarian. Discouraging use not only violates the "Books are for use" maxim but also undermines the leadership status of the librarian.

Every Reader His Book

The literacy goals of a school can only be reached if there are appropriate materials available for each student, and the school librarian leads this effort in a variety of ways. To provide a wide range of reading experiences from print and digital sources, the school librarian's collection development procedure requires intimate familiarity with the school's official curriculum—codified in school or district documents—and unofficial curriculum—the curriculum actually taught by each individual teacher. The school librarian develops personal relationships with teachers to learn curricular preferences and teaching styles and collects materials to support and extend that curriculum. The librarian's participation on curriculum development teams also affords opportunities to understand resource needs and to have some influence on how such resources get used, assuring that students are matched with learning resources as effectively as possible.

Collection development for school libraries is different than for public libraries; the responsibility of acting *in loco parentis* constrains school librarians and provides parents and other members of the school community with some leverage over collection choices. Nevertheless, as the American Library Association document

"Access to Resources and Services in the School Library Media Program: An Interpretation of the Library Bill of Rights" (available at http://www.ala.org/) states,

Members of the school community involved in the collection development process employ educational criteria to select resources unfettered by their personal, political, social, or religious views. Students and educators served by the school library media program have access to resources and services free of constraints resulting from personal, partisan, or doctrinal disapproval. School library media specialists resist efforts by individuals or groups to define what is appropriate for all students or teachers to read, view, hear, or access via electronic means.

As a literacy leader striving for the goal of "every reader his book," the school librarian educates the school community about the need to collect for every segment of the school population, pushing back against the inclination to restrict the collection to the lowest common denominators of interest and standards of acceptability.

Enlisting the participation of other leaders in the school community—including parents, teachers, administrators and school board members—in the creation of a formal collection development policy and materials challenge process is an effective way of communicating the vision of a collection which serves the needs of an entire school population. Creation of such policies not only helps smooth disagreements over materials; these policies can change the understanding about a school collection in ways that may ward off disagreements in the first place.

Even in the way a school collection is organized, the school librarian can take a leadership role. There is evidence from both school and public libraries to suggest, for example, that organizing a fiction collection by genre instead of alphabetically by author will increase circulation (Dumas 2005; Shepherd and Baker 1987; Stiles 2004). In recent years, public and school libraries have taken cues from bookstores, placing priority on product placement and rearranging collections to make popular materials more accessible.

Nothing substitutes, though, for simply having a wide variety of reading materials available for students wherever they go. In *What Really Matters for Struggling Readers: Designing Research-Based Programs* (2003), Richard Allington recommends students spend at least 90 minutes a day reading in school, as well as that significant effort be placed on students reading the "just right" material. In *The Power of Reading*, Krashen (2004) reviews a body of research supporting the idea that the more reading resources available, the more students will read, and the more students read, the higher their academic achievement. A proponent of free voluntary reading, Krashen suggests that "the most obvious step" in this activity is "to provide access to books" (57); he also says that the key to providing access is the strength of the school library, including the size of the collection, its circulation policies, and the availability of resources for student and staff use. The school librarian can exert leadership here by pushing for higher acquisitions budgets and by helping teachers create classroom collections that include high-interest fiction and nonfiction, newspapers and magazines, poetry, drama, and content area trade books. Rather than stagnate within one room, such collections can be designed, with the help of library staff, to rotate from one classroom to the next, to the library, and back to classrooms.

In a digital context, "every book his reader" raises further challenges for the school librarian. Leadership here means staying current with the shifting formats, applications, and hardware, as well as being prudent about what technologies and platforms to invest in heavily and what to merely sample. Even a resource as seemingly straightforward as audiobooks creates a string of questions: Do we purchase PlayAways? Do we make books available as downloads to an MP3 player? If we only have a choice between MP3 and iPod formats, which should we choose? In addition, it is largely up to the school librarian to help both students and the rest of the school community see both the value and the joy of such resources as audiobooks, videos, simulations, and other digital content. Introducing new resources in new formats requires not just the purchase and display of materials, but active campaigns to make students and staff aware of their availability and to train those who need extra help. In some cases, administrators and school boards need to be convinced that the new technology actually contributes to student learning. Even resources as widely adopted as audiobooks meet with skepticism in some school cultures. Assessing the school climate and creating a plan to advance digital resources is part of literacy leadership.

Creating and sustaining collections that serve the diverse needs of a school community are fundamental in the school librarian's role as literacy leader. Careful planning, listening to students and staff, and promoting both systems and resources help the school librarian advance the literacy goals of the library program, ensuring Ranganathan's maxims, "Books [and other resources] are for use" and "Every book [or audio book, or video, or Web site, or interactive game, or other resource] his reader."

PART IV: WORKING WITH THE SCHOOL SITE AND DISTRICT TO CREATE COMPLEMENTARY GOALS

Every educator is concerned about literacy, and the focus on testing in the past decade has intensified this concern. In 2005, the National Association of Secondary School Principals published a document entitled *Creating a Culture of Literacy: A Guide for Middle and High School Principals*, a detailed roadmap for addressing literacy at the secondary level. In 122 pages, the word "library" is mentioned just twice—once in reference to classroom libraries and once in relation to funding for stronger collections. The word "librarian" is only mentioned in the bibliography.

From the vantage point of school librarianship as a profession, this type of document is a monumental failure of literacy leadership. School librarians are instructional leaders; in an area as fundamental as literacy, their instructional leadership should be evident to everyone in a school community. Such leadership, though, is not conferred, but earned. In 2007, Lance, Rodney, and Russell reported in a study of Indiana school libraries that almost 90 percent of principals' knowledge of the school librarian's role came from experience on the job. In other words, principals are not told school librarians are literacy leaders; they only learn this when school librarians take up the charge.

School librarians on leadership, curriculum, and professional development committees are in a position to advocate for a focus on literacy and to include into the planning documents of a school or district specific roles the library program will fill in meeting literacy goals. Familiarity with a school's data—statewide reading scores, school- and course-wide assessments, course grades—is a tremendous asset. The school librarian can use such data to identify both literacy-related strengths and areas for improvement in student performance, as well as help other school leaders recognize both the current role and the potential the library program holds to strengthen literacy gains.

If a curriculum planning committee decides, for example, that students need more instruction and practice identifying the main idea, the school librarian might suggest a strategy such as paragraph shrinking (Fuchs, Fuchs, and Burish 2000)—a reciprocal teaching activity in which students read aloud to each other and "shrink" the paragraph down to 10 words most important about the "who" or "what" of the paragraph. The school librarian might offer to provide instruction to classroom teachers about how to implement the strategy and locate high-interest materials related to several areas of the curriculum for teachers to use with their students in practicing the strategy. Classes conducting research in the library might use a note-taking form that includes a version of paragraph shrinking. In this example, the specific role the school librarian plays in helping to strengthen literacy arises from a need identified by school-wide data.

At schools where students have low reading scores, leaders can be reminded of studies showing the summer gap is a real phenomenon and that one of the best remedies is a thoughtful summer reading program (Allington and McGill-Franzen 2003). Even at schools with predominantly good reading scores, the librarian can share research showing that regardless of background or ability, students who read during the summer outperform those who do not when they return to school in the fall (Kim 2004). Such studies provide a perfect introduction to a school librarian's proposal for a summer reading program managed through the school library program.

Of course, standardized test scores are woefully inadequate in measuring the range of skills students need to thrive after high school in the twenty-first century. Working knowledge of major literacy initiatives—those at the state and national levels—is equally important for the school librarian as literacy leader. When a new initiative is introduced, it is helpful to comb that document for specific recommendations or observations that might be addressed in a substantive way through the school library program.

For example, included among the 15 major elements of a healthy literacy curriculum identified in *Reading Next: A Vision for Action and Research in Middle and High School Literacy* (Snow and Biancarosa 2004) are these 4 which clearly suggest a role for the school library program:

- Motivation and self-directed learning, which includes building motivation to read and learn and providing students with the instruction and supports needed for independent learning tasks they will face after graduation
- Text-based collaborative learning, which involves students interacting with one another around a variety of texts
- Diverse texts, which are texts at a variety of difficulty levels and on a variety of topics
- A technology component, which includes technology as a tool for and a topic of literacy instruction

If the curriculum or staff development team uses this document as part of its planning, a school librarian who is a literacy leader will have previewed the recommendations and sketched out specific ideas about how the school library will play an integral part in addressing these curricular issues. If such a document is not used directly by a planning team, the school librarian may still draw on it for support of the library's role in addressing the school-wide literacy goals. A school with a large English Language Learner population may not be focusing on the 2007 report *Double the Work: Challenges and*

Solutions to Acquiring Language and Academic Literacy for Adolescent English Language Learners (Short and Fitzsimmons), but the document's emphasis on building background knowledge, integration of technology into literacy instruction, use of multimedia materials, and motivation of students through choice of a wide range of reading materials all indicate a central role for the school library program.

Studies and reports that garner national attention are among the most valuable resources available to a school librarian for focusing attention on multiple literacies and the importance of technology in their development. The 2009 Horizon Report (Johnson, Levine, and Smith), for example, offers five critical challenges for education. The first two speak directly to literacy and the role a school library program may play in our information-rich world:

- There is a growing need for formal instruction in key new skills, including information literacy, visual literacy, and technological literacy.
- Students are different, but a lot of educational material is not. Schools are still using materials developed decades ago, but today's students come to school with very different experiences than those of 20 or 30 years ago, and think and work very differently as well.

The school librarian who joins curriculum and staff development planning teams at the school or district level makes no assumptions about other literacy leaders' understanding of the role the school library program plays in a school community. Armed with school-wide data, best practice research, and recommendations from major literacy initiatives, the school librarian is positioned to help frame how literacy issues will be addressed and to help others understand the critical role the school library program plays in advancing literacy goals.

PART V: BECOMING A LITERACY EXPERT AND SHARING KNOWLEDGE WITH STAFF

While there are many paths to becoming a literacy leader, all require that the school librarian gain a deep understanding of the reading and writing processes, of the best practices for teaching literacy skills across the curriculum, of the role technology plays in literacy instruction and learning, and of best practice in the ways school librarians contribute to student literacy gains.

Where does one start this journey of a thousand miles? Among the best sources for current thinking on literacy issues are professional organizations and their journals, including the International Reading Association (*The Reading Teacher, Journal of Adolescent & Adult Literacy, Reading Research Quarterly Online*), National Council of Teachers of English (*Language Arts, Voices from the Middle, English Journal*), and the National Reading Conference (*Journal of Literacy Research*). For addressing the intersection between school library programs and literacy, membership in the American Association of School Librarians and subscription to its journal, *Knowledge Quest*, is mandatory. For literacy leadership perspectives outside the school library, the Association for Supervision and Curriculum Development, its journal *Educational Leadership*, and many of its professional publications offer both practical approaches and theoretical underpinnings. The point here is simply to start and to acknowledge that literacy leadership requires an ongoing commitment to one's own literacy education.

In the course of such reading, one will encounter a core set of texts that are widely influential in professionals' thinking about literacy, including

- Allen, J. 2000. *Yellow brick roads: Shared and guided paths to independent reading 4–12.* York, ME: Stenhouse.
- Allington, R. 2003. *What really matters for struggling readers: Designing research-based programs.* New York: Addison-Wesley Longman.
- Atwell, N. 1998. *In the middle: New understandings about writing, reading and learning* (2nd ed.). Portsmouth, NH: Heinemann-Boynton/Cook.
- Atwell, N. 2007. *The reading zone: How to help kids become skilled, passionate, habitual, critical readers.* New York: Scholastic Professional Books.
- Burke, J. 2000. *Reading reminders: Tools, tips and techniques.* Portsmouth, NH: Boynton/Cook.
- Calkins, L. 1994. *The art of teaching writing* (2nd ed.). Portsmouth, NH: Heinemann.
- Calkins, L. 2000. *The art of teaching reading.* Portsmouth, NH: Heinemann.
- Coiro, J., M. Knobel, C. Lankshear, and D. Leu, eds. 2009. *Handbook of research on new literacies.* Mahwah, NJ: Erlbaum.
- Daniels, H. 2002. *Literature circles: Voice and choice in book clubs and reading groups* (2nd ed.). Portland, ME: Stenhouse.
- Fountas, I., and G. Pinnell. 1996. *Guided reading: Good first teaching for all children.* Portsmouth, NH: Heinemann.
- Gregory, G., and L. Kuzmich. 2005. *Differentiated literacy strategies for student growth and achievement in grades K–6.* Thousand Oaks, CA: Corwin Press.
- Harvey, S., and A. Goudvis. 2007. *Strategies that work: Teaching comprehension for understanding and engagement* (2nd ed.). Portland, ME: Stenhouse.
- Keene, E. O., and S. Zimmermann. 2007. *Mosaic of thought: The power of comprehension strategy instruction* (2nd ed.). Portsmouth, NH: Heinemann.
- Krashen, S. D. 2004. *The power of reading: Insights from the research.* Westport, CT: Libraries Unlimited, Heinemann.
- Tovani, C. 2000. *I read it, but I don't get it: Comprehension strategies for adolescent readers.* Portland, ME: Stenhouse.
- Trelease, J. 2001. *The read-aloud handbook* (6th ed.). New York: Penguin Books.
- Vacca, R. T., and J. L. Vacca. 2005. *Content area reading: Literacy and learning across the curriculum* (8th ed.). Glenview, IL: Scott, Foresman and Company.
- Wilhelm, J. D. 2007. *Engaging readers & writers with inquiry: Promoting deep understandings in language arts and the content areas with guiding questions (theory and practice).* New York: Scholastic Professional Books.

These books are valuable in creating a foundational understanding of the reading and writing processes and the theoretical models of the relationships among reader, writer, and text. They also offer a stockpile of best-practice strategies for teaching reading and writing, which can become one of the school librarian's greatest assets in promoting both the library program and a school's literacy goals. Most teachers, it should be noted, acquire very little literacy training in their pre-service programs (Mather, Bos, and Babur 2001; Nouri and Lenski 1998; Stewart and O'Brien 1989).

A workshop introducing Stephanie Harvey and Anne Goudvis's strategy of making connections between personal experience and text (2007) may lead to a deepened relationship between classroom teacher and librarian in locating texts that lend themselves to this learning. A meeting with science teachers about offering students choice in their reading for a curricular unit could blossom into deeper collaborations with that department or to expanded use of trade books and periodical databases. Working with English teachers to explore the connections between the reading, writing, and inquiry processes may lead to more use of library resources and instructional design that deepens students' literacy skills.

When a staff comes to identify the librarian as a literacy leader with genuine instructional expertise, teacher contacts with the librarian increase. Some of these contacts will just be a search for advice—which pre-reading strategy to use, how to increase engagement with a particular text, how to run a peer-editing session—but other contacts will lead to increased instructional collaboration and an increased integration of the library program into the literacy curriculum of the school. As teachers build their own literacy expertise with the mentorship of the librarian, they come to understand more fully why the library program is an essential component in students' literacy development.

PART VI: COLLABORATING WITH TEACHERS TO PLAN, TEACH, AND EVALUATE LESSONS THAT PROMOTE LITERACY

One of the most enduring impacts a school librarian can have on a classroom teacher occurs during collaborations, in which the librarian models good instructional design, effective teaching strategies, classroom management, and meaningful assessments. When collaborating with classroom teachers to plan, teach, and evaluate lessons, the librarian has an opportunity to promote and push literacy goals. In any given activity, the librarian might ask a teacher a number of questions related to helping students into, through, and beyond the texts they encounter, such as:

- What should we do to prepare the students for the reading and writing they will do?
- What kind of scaffolds should we provide students to help them through this content or process?
- How can we help students make connections between this reading or writing and other content they have already encountered?
- How can we get the students to read or write just a little bit more?

As a literacy leader, the school librarian is ready in collaborations with teachers to ask questions and suggest strategies that allow classroom teachers to integrate literacy instruction seamlessly into the content of their courses. The librarian's knowledge of individual teaching styles and abilities comes into play here too, of course. The traditional, students-in-a-row/sage-on-the-stage teacher may not be ready for the group work required of literature circles but may be ready for a graphic organizer to help students take more effective notes from their reading and research. The experimenter and risk-taker, on the other hand, may be ready to jump into explorations of new technologies and new literacies on a moment's notice.

Effectively introducing a new literacy concept or strategy into a classroom teacher's lesson creates ripples far beyond what takes place in that single collaboration. The teacher who observes how students are motivated when they have some choice over what they read will be more likely to offer choice on other assignments.

The teacher who sees how much better his students negotiate new content after a well-planned pre-reading activity will incorporate similar activities into his classroom teaching. Such one-on-one collaborations offer powerful opportunities for change and growth. A school librarian who weaves a deep understanding of literacy issues into frequent instructional collaborations with teachers will influence literacy instruction among entire teaching staffs and contribute to the literacy gains of hundreds or even thousands of students each year.

PART VII: DEEPENING OUR UNDERSTANDING OF HOW LITERACY IS CHANGING

The traditional leadership roles of the school librarian discussed in preceding pages remain vital. But technology has fundamentally changed the definition of literacy, and school librarians are among those at a school site best positioned to lead explorations and help school communities consider the ramifications of that change, as well as to develop educational approaches that effectively exploit technologies and build new literacy skills.

In the *Handbook of Research on New Literacies*, Coiro, Knobel, Lankshear, and Leu (2009) offer four interrelated factors that have changed the nature of literacy. First is the ubiquity of the Internet. Recent Pew studies indicate that 74 percent of adults use the Internet in the United States; among those adults under 30, that number rises to 87 percent (Pew Internet & American Life Project 2008), while 94 percent of teens use the Internet (Lenhart et al. 2008). Globally, the growth of Internet users has increased nearly 300 percent since 2000, from about 360 million to almost 1.6 billion users (Internet World Stats 2009). Second, the nature of the Internet itself allows for the continuous change of literacy technologies themselves (Coiro et al. 2009). Not only does the ubiquity of the Internet allow for the rapid dissemination of new technologies, but the potentials within internet technology continue to spawn new technologies, including blogs, wikis, instant messaging, video and music sharing technologies, and even improvements to older technologies such as word processing. Third, such technologies, say Coiro, Knobel, Lankshear, and Leu, "change the form and functions of earlier literacies since they carry within them new potentials for literacy" (2009, 5). The implications of these three developments together create a fourth factor: "literacy is no longer a static construct from the standpoint of its defining technology for the past 500 years; it has now come to mean a rapid and continuous process of change in the ways in which we read, write, view, listen, compose and communicate information" (5).

Perhaps the most important illustration of the way information and communication technologies have changed literacy deals specifically with the issue of reading comprehension. Reading comprehension models typically include a whole range of elements a reader brings to the table when engaging with a text, including background knowledge, schema, a level of engagement—as well as a range of skills, such as decoding, predicting, questioning, visualizing, identifying important ideas, drawing conclusions, and monitoring one's own comprehension. In a qualitative study of 11 adolescent readers, Coiro and Dobler (2007) present a compelling case that online reading requires similar but more complex processes for successful comprehension. The unbounded nature of the Internet is a principal reason for this difference; while print reading tends to be linear and finite, the Internet allows an infinite number of choices about where to venture next. With each choice about what to click on or what to search for, readers participate in the creation of new, unique texts. The text is not a static work presented by a single author but a collection of works by any number of contributors, including, in a Web 2.0 environment, the reader himself. In such a scenario, reading comprehension is not only a function of the reader's background knowledge, decoding skills, disposition, and meta-cognitive strategies employed in negotiating a single print text; reading comprehension also depends upon the critical choices the reader makes about what to click on, when to search for clarifying or confirming information, how to navigate the schema of a Web page, how to use a search engine, and how to evaluate the reliability of an information source (Coiro and Dobler 2007, Dalton and Proctor 2009, Dobler 2007).

In addition, processes also used while reading print text become more complex. A recent study indicates that students who were given content-specific background-building information prior to their Internet reading activity actually performed more complex navigational tasks in search of information than did a control group (Lawless, Schrader, and Mayall 2007). Background knowledge, in other words, may influence the quality of searching the reader conducts. Accessing prior knowledge, others suggest, may also now include not only one's understanding of the content but of organizational structures on the Web, use of specific search tools, and an understanding of which type of resources may best address a question (Coiro 2007, Coiro and Dobler 2007).

Studies comparing online and print reading processes indicate, in fact, that some adolescents who score high on traditional print reading comprehension tests may score low in an online reading test, and vice versa (Coiro 2007, Coiro and Dobler 2007, Leu et al. 2007). Several important implications arise from these studies. First, the fact that some students who score poorly in traditional print reading comprehension tests score well in online tests suggests that there are additional compensatory reading strategies available in an online environment that may be of benefit to struggling readers. Second, while there are many overlapping skills involved in reading online and in print, the processes are not isomorphic. Leu et al. (2007) call the Internet "the defining technology for literacy and learning in the twenty-first century" (49). Whether or not this proves to be true, understanding the unique processes involved in online reading comprehension is more critical than ever.

It is in the definition of this reading process that the leadership role of the school librarian comes into focus. Several proponents of new literacies have identified five major functions involved with online reading comprehension (Coiro 2007, Coiro et al. 2009, Leu et al. 2007):

1. Identifying important questions
2. Locating information
3. Analyzing information
4. Synthesizing information
5. Communicating information

School librarians will recognize these functions as critical components of information literacy—now being absorbed into a broader conception of the general term of literacy. In describing these functions, Leu et al. (2007) write that they "contain the skills, strategies, and dispositions that are both distinctive to online reading comprehension and, at the same time, appear to overlap somewhat with offline reading comprehension" (45). This language will also sound familiar to those who have read and considered the American Association of School Librarians' *Standards for the 21st-Century Learner* (2007), which is organized around key pursuits that require specific skills, strategies, dispositions, and a fourth component, responsibilities.

What used to fall under the domain of information literacy—a territory traditionally claimed by school librarians—has been absorbed into a broader conception of literacy. In some ways, this can be a boon for school librarians who have struggled to create a common language between themselves and classroom teachers, who seldom, if ever, encounter the term "information literacy" in their own disciplines. Everybody—not just teachers but administrators, students, parents, school board members, legislators, the press—believes literacy is a cornerstone of lifelong learning.

The disorienting shift educators must make in accepting the notion of "new literacies" is that in some respects, teachers may be less literate than their students. Leu et al. (2007) expand on this idea:

As ever newer literacies appear and fragment our literacy landscape, it should be increasingly expected that at least one student always knows more than any teacher about some aspect of online reading comprehension. New models of instruction need to take advantage of this intellectual capital that will be increasingly distributed around a classroom—the new literacies that students possess and that teachers may not. (49)

Far from obviating teachers, though, the Internet and the expanding array of Web 2.0 technologies, including wikis, blogs, and social networking sites, require increased focus on the critical evaluation of source and content. The challenge for the school librarian as a new literacy leader is twofold: to help the school community understand the need to expand our traditional notions of literacy to include new literacies, and to lead, through study, communication, staff development, curricular planning, and collaboration with classroom teachers, the exploration of new literacies, examining current research and trying promising strategies that may lead to best practice.

The *Handbook of Research on New Literacies* (Coiro et al. 2009) provides a research foundation for thinking about literacy in new ways; several contributors to this collection are also part of the New Literacies Research Team at the University of Connecticut (http://www.newliteracies.uconn.edu). The Partnership for 21st Century Skills (http://www.21stcenturyskills.org) has created perhaps the most sensible framework and a set of content-area skills maps to show what such learning looks like at the elementary, middle, and high school levels. The 21st Century Information Fluency Project, begun at the Illinois Mathematics and Science Academy, provides resources for both educators and students that incorporate new literacy concepts into specific teaching and learning activities. David Warlick's *Redefining Literacy 2.0* (2009) offers reflections and examples of what literacy teaching and learning look like in a technology- and information-rich environment. Warlick makes a point that school librarians might repeat often: while many educators talk about the need to integrate technology into the curriculum, we should instead focus on the integration of literacy:

If we can rethink what it is to be literate in today's information environment, and integrate that, then the technology will come. . . . Computers and the internet will be an essential part of teaching and learning because they are the tools of contemporary literacy. (xiii)

These are but a few of the resources school librarians might investigate in expanding their literacy leadership roles to include new literacies. The extent to which school librarians can facilitate their school communities' framing of information and communication skills within the broader context of literacy will surely influence the school library program's impact on teaching and learning.

CONCLUSION

Literacy is a cornerstone of lifelong learning, central not only to the purpose of a school library but to K–12 education itself. Literacy leadership begins with a vision: what literacy issues does the school or district need to be focusing on in its teaching and learning? The school librarian's vision is then communicated through other acts of leadership, including promoting a love of reading and collecting and organizing a diverse collection for maximum access and use. Participation in curriculum and professional development planning affords the school librarian opportunities to further articulate a literacy vision and help other school leaders understand the vital role a school library plays in building literacy. Leading literacy workshops and collaborating with classroom teachers—activities informed by an expanding base of knowledge from the school librarian's own professional development—inculcates others into a culture of literacy and learning that drives the original vision. With expertise in information literacy and more technology- and information-rich teaching experience than most others on a school campus, the school librarian is naturally positioned to lead explorations of technology's impact on literacy. At schools without such leadership, school libraries run the risk of becoming irrelevant. At schools with librarians who are true literacy leaders, though, school libraries can become pivotal in twenty-first-century literacy learning.

REFERENCES

Allington, R., and A. McGill-Franzen. 2003. The impact of summer setback on the reading achievement gap. *Phi Delta Kappan* 85 (1): 68–75.

American Association of School Librarians. 2007. *Standards for the 21st-century learner.* Chicago: American Library Association.

Bodart, J. 1985. *Booktalk! 2: Booktalking for all ages and audiences.* New York: Wilson.

Cart, M. 2007. Teacher-librarian as literacy leader. *Teacher Librarian* 34 (3): 8–12.

Cipielewski, J., and K. E. Stanovich. 1992. Predicting growth in reading ability from children's exposure to print. *Journal of Experimental Child Psychology* 54: 74–89.

Coiro, J. 2007. Exploring changes to reading comprehension on the Internet: Paradoxes and possibilities for diverse adolescent readers. Doctoral dissertation. University of Connecticut.

Coiro, J., and E. Dobler. 2007. Exploring the online reading comprehension strategies used by sixth-grade skilled readers to search for and locate information on the Internet. *Reading Research Quarterly* 42 (2): 214–257.

Coiro, J., M. Knobel, C. Lankshear, and D. Leu. 2009. Central issues in new literacies. In *Handbook of research on new literacies*, eds. J. Coiro, M. Knobel, C. Lankshear, and D. Leu, 1–21. Mahwah, NJ: Erlbaum.

———, eds. 2009. *Handbook of research on new literacies.* Mahwah, NJ: Erlbaum.

Cunningham, A. E., and K. E. Stanovich. 1991. Tracking the unique effects of print exposure in children: Associations with vocabulary, general knowledge and spelling. *Journal of Educational Psychology* 83: 264–274.

Dalton, B., and C. P. Proctor. 2009. The changing landscape of text and comprehension in the age of new literacies. In *Handbook of research on new literacies*, eds. J. Coiro, M. Knobel, C. Lankshear, and D. Leu, 297–324. Mahwah, NJ: Erlbaum.

Dobler, E. 2007. Reading the Web: The merging of literacy and technology. In *School reform and the school library media specialist*, eds. S. Hughes-Hassell and V. H. Harada, 93–110. Westport, CT: Libraries Unlimited.

Dumas, E. P. 2005. Give 'em what they want! Reorganizing your fiction collection by genre. *Library Media Connection* 24 (2): 20–22.

Fargo, L. 1931. School libraries in the United States. *Peabody Journal of Education* 8 (4): 236–240.

Fuchs, D., L. S. Fuchs, and P. Burish. 2000. Peer-assisted learning strategies: An evidence-based practice to promote reading achievement. *Learning Disabilities Research & Practice* 15 (2): 85–91.

Guthrie, J. T., and C. H. Schafer. 2001. Benefits of opportunity to read and balanced instruction on the NAEP. *The Journal of Educational Research* 94 (3): 145–163.

Harvey, S., and A. Goudvis. 2007. *Strategies that work: Teaching comprehension for understanding and engagement* (2nd ed.). Portland, ME: Stenhouse.

Honnold, R. 2002. *101+ teen programs that work*. New York: Neal-Schuman.

———. 2005. *More teen programs that work*. New York: Neal-Schuman.

Internet World Stats. 2009. *World Internet users and population stats*. http://www.internetworldstats .com/stats.htm (accessed January 5, 2009).

Johnson, L., A. Levine, and R. Smith. 2009. *The 2009 Horizon Report*. Austin, TX: The New Media Consortium.

Kim, J. 2004. Summer reading and the ethnic achievement gap. *Journal of Education for Students Placed at Risk* 9 (2): 169–188.

Krashen, Stephen. 2004. *The power of reading*. Westport, CT: Libraries Unlimited and Heinemann.

Krisch, I., J. deJong, D. LaFonain, J. MacQueen, J. Mendelovits, and C. Moneur. 2002. *Reading for change: Performance and engagement across countries: Results from PISA 2000*. Paris, France: Center for Educational Research, Organization for Economic Co-operation and Development.

Lance, K. C., M. J. Rodney, and B. Russell. 2007. *How students, teachers, and principals benefit from strong school libraries: The Indiana study*. Indianapolis, IN: Association for Indiana Media Educators.

Lawless, K. A., P. G. Schrader, and H. J. Mayall. 2007. Acquisition of information online: Knowledge, navigation and learning outcomes. *Journal of Literacy Research* 39 (3): 289–306.

Lenhart, A., S. Arafeh, A. Smith, and A. Rankin Macgill. 2008. Writing, technology and teens. Pew Internet & American Life Project. http://www.pewinternet.org/PPF/r/247/report _display.asp (accessed January 14, 2009).

Leu, D. J., L. Zawilinski, J. Castek, M. Banerjee, B. Housand, Y. Liu, and M. O'Neil. 2007. What is new about the new literacies of online reading comprehension? In *Secondary school reading and writing: What research reveals for classroom practices*, eds. A. Berger, L. Rush, and J. Eakle, 37–68. Chicago: National Council of Teachers of English/National Conference of Research on Language and Literacy.

Mather, N., C. Bos, and N. Babur. 2001. Perceptions and knowledge of preservice and inservice teachers about early literacy instruction. *Journal of Learning Disabilities* 24 (5): 472–482.

McAndrew, D. A. 2005. *Literacy leadership: Six strategies for peoplework*. Newark, DE: International Reading Association.

National Association of Secondary School Principals. 2005. *Creating a culture of literacy: A guide for middle and high school principals.* Reston, VA: National Association of Secondary School Principals.

Nouri, B. L., and S. D. Lenski. 1998. The (in)effectiveness of content area literacy instruction. *Clearing House* 71 (6): 372–374.

Ranganathan, S. R. 1931. *The five laws of library science.* London: Madras Library Association. http://dlist.sir.arizona.edu/1220/ (accessed December 27, 2008).

Shepherd, G. W., and S. L. Baker. 1987. Fiction classification: A brief review of the research. *Public Libraries* 26: 31–32.

Short, D., and S. Fitzsimmons. 2007. *Double the work: Challenges and solutions to acquiring language and academic literacy for adolescent English language learners.* New York: Carnegie Corporation and Alliance for Excellent Education.

Snow, C., and G. Biancarosa. 2004. *Reading next: A vision for action and research in middle and high school literacy.* Washington, DC: Alliance for Excellent Education.

Stewart, R. A., and D. G. O'Brien. 1989. Resistance to content area reading: A focus on preservice teachers. *Journal of Reading* 32 (5): 396–401.

Stiles, L. 2004. Shelf shifters. *School Library Journal* 50 (9): 32.

Warlick, D. 2009. *Redefining literacy 2.0* (2nd ed.). Columbus, OH: Linworth Books.

6

The Teacher-Librarian as a Curriculum Leader

Jody K. Howard

INTRODUCTION

Carol and Tammy are both teacher-librarians in elementary schools in a large suburban school district. The district department responsible for the English/language arts curriculum decided to implement a new district-wide curriculum in the K–6 schools. This curriculum was extremely structured and had the teachers monitoring the students' instructional time for each activity. The curriculum did not identify any time for research or provide the students with an opportunity to check out books of interest. The staff at both schools explained to Carol and Tammy that the students could not be scheduled into the library for any collaborative lessons or book checkout because of the new curriculum. Carol became extremely stressed and indicated that this was the end of her program. Tammy worked with the teachers and explained how the structured curriculum made her role even more essential in the development and implementation of the curriculum.

What is the difference in these two examples? Both teacher-librarians were professionally trained, and both had good programs to this point. Why was there such a difference in their responses? The answer is simple. Tammy used her leadership skills to determine how she could still align her program with the new curriculum. She also called upon the personal relationships she had with the faculty members to show she is a team player, an integral part to the implementation of the curriculum. Carol, on the other hand, saw the curriculum for what it was and did not reflect on a creative solution as to how she could still work with the teachers for the academic achievement of the students. Both of the teacher-librarians had the good of the students and staff at heart, but only Tammy understood how she must use her leadership skills to fulfill her curriculum role for the advancement of the students.

Many thanks to Nadine Abrahams, teacher-librarian at Westview Elementary in Northglenn, Colorado, for sharing her curriculum expertise for this chapter.

Teacher-librarians have many roles associated with their positions. Exhibiting leadership in the curriculum area is one role which is sometimes overlooked. Working with and being involved in the development and implementation of curriculum is often misunderstood.

The purpose of this chapter is to examine this role and to discuss how the teacher-librarian demonstrates leadership in curriculum at the school level and extends this leadership influence to the district, state, and national levels. In beginning this discussion, it is important to have an idea of what leadership is and what qualities a teacher-librarian must develop in order to exhibit leadership specifically in the area of curriculum development and implementation.

LEADERSHIP—INITIAL THOUGHTS

A review of the professional literature shows that many works discuss that teacher-librarians must be leaders and exhibit leadership qualities (Lance, Rodney, and Hamilton-Pennell 2000; Howard and Eckhardt 2005; Harvey 2008; Zmuda and Harada 2008; American Association of School Librarians [AASL] 2009). Leadership is intangible and is described in various ways. Bennis (2003) indicates that there are more than 850 definitions of leadership. Many of the definitions have withstood the test of time and many simply describe the qualities that make a leader. Woolls (1990) uses a simple definition, stating that leadership should be examined from the verb form of "lead." Leaders are ones who lead other people or move people in certain directions. Spillane, Halverson, and Diamond (2004) see innovation and acting as a change agent as necessary components of leadership.

To better understand the qualities the teacher-librarian needs to become a leader in the area of curriculum, it is important to examine what this role includes, beginning with an awareness of what curriculum includes and how the teacher-librarian and curriculum are related. This review will lay a foundation for the skills that are needed to implement and bring this role to fruition.

WHAT IS CURRICULUM?

When entering the field of education, one of the first words that a practitioner encounters is "curriculum." This word describes much of what occurs in the classroom setting. Curriculum includes the teacher-prepared lessons presented every day, the guides that explain the content of the class, the scope of the subject matter, and the sequence of when and how the information is presented. It identifies the methods of teaching the course, the duration of the course, the necessary resources, and the proposed materials used for instruction. The word also describes entire programs that present educational materials with a specific focus, such as the reading curriculum, the English curriculum, or the math curriculum. "Curriculum" is a general word that encompasses myriad aspects of the educational process (Eisenberg and Berkowitz 1988).

The teacher-librarian's role in the K–12 school is intertwined with the school's curriculum. This role has changed over the years as the image of the teacher-librarian has evolved. The teacher-librarian's role at the school level is a necessary ingredient for the academic success of the students. In analyzing this role, it is necessary to examine it in relation to the support provided to the teacher in the classroom and to understand that the teacher-librarian has the responsibility of addressing a variety of literacies: information, media, visual, and technology (AASL 2007). At the school level, the teacher-librarian must be an information specialist and an instructional partner (AASL 2009). Teacher-librarians are curriculum consultants, curriculum supporters, curriculum aligners, and curriculum developers. Each of these roles entails different responsibilities and skills to be accomplished effectively. In addition to the school roles, the teacher-librarian has a responsibility to address curriculum issues at the district, state, and the national levels.

What needs to be implemented in order to make certain teacher-librarians become the information specialists and curriculum designers, as stated by *Information Power: Guidelines for School Library Media Programs* (AASL and Association for Educational Communications and Technology 1988), *Information Power: Building Partnerships for Learning* (AASL and Association for Educational Communications and Technology 1998), and *Empowering Learners* (AASL 2009)? The bottom line is that the teacher-librarian needs to understand the content of the curriculum, the content standards, the library collection, and the current standards derived from the *Standards for the 21st-Century Learner* (AASL 2007). In addition, teacher-librarians must understand how teachers think when they are developing curriculum, how the curriculum is developed, and the purpose of the curriculum. The teacher-librarian must have certain technical skills at his or her disposal and, most assuredly, must employ definitive leadership skills to become the information specialist.

INFORMATION SPECIALIST—CURRICULUM CONTENT

The national standards, state standards, and the district interpretation of these standards describe the curriculum presented in the classroom. The standards provide good frameworks for the knowledge the teachers need to present to the students, and the teacher-librarian needs to understand these standards. The challenge in studying the curriculum standards is the vast amount of knowledge that they address. Marzano, Kendall, and Gaddy (as cited in Marzano, Waters, and McNulty 2005) have concluded that in examining the content standards and tabulating the amount of time needed to present the information addressed by the standards, teachers would need to increase the amount of instructional contact time by 71 percent. Marzano, Waters, and McNulty (2005) continue by explaining that in order to be exposed to all of the content in the standards with the school year timeframe remaining as it is today, students would need to continue their schooling for an additional 10 years. The authors advocate having a viable curriculum, one that can be presented in the allotted timeframe of the existing school year. Working with their colleagues and district administrators, classroom teachers have determined what the essential content is that constitutes a viable curriculum and needs to be addressed during the school year. The teacher-librarian needs to know what this curriculum includes at the school level and in each classroom in the school.

Zweizig and Hopkins (1999) identify three types of curriculum. The intended curriculum contains the goals and objects found in district frameworks, guidelines, and textbooks dedicated to the specific subject area. The implemented curriculum is what the teachers actually teach during the school year, and the assessed curriculum is the content found on state and standardized tests. The teacher-librarian must have knowledge in all of these areas: what the district frameworks include, what the teachers actually teach, and the content on the state and local assessments.

The teacher-librarian has access to the state standards through the state education Web site and should be familiar with the parameters of the documents. Frameworks for the district curriculum are also available through the district central office and Web site. The teacher-librarian should obtain copies of these documents for his or her use and, after studying the documents, should make them available in the library. Armed with the knowledge of the curriculum standards, the teacher-librarian should begin general conversations with the classroom teachers concerning what content is taught in the classroom.

The goal of having this knowledge is so the teacher-librarian will provide the resource and instructional support that a teacher needs to implement the curriculum. Two tools are available to assist the teacher-librarian in determining what support is needed: curriculum mapping and collection mapping.

INFORMATION SPECIALIST—CURRICULUM MAPPING

Heidi Jacobs (1997) has provided extensive information in the area of curriculum mapping. This process involves looking at each class and determining what is actually being taught during the school year. One important aspect of curriculum mapping is making certain that each classroom teacher has an individual curriculum map, as all teachers assigned to teach the same material do not necessarily cover the same content during the school year. A curriculum map is not what is *supposed* to be taught but what is *actually* taught. The district guidelines and curriculum frameworks detail what should be taught, but they seldom reflect what happens day by day in the classroom. A teacher may have a favorite unit that he or she would like to teach that is outside of the curriculum framework. One teacher-librarian in a middle school received a request each year to send all of her Holocaust materials used in the eighth grade curriculum to a specific elementary school. One fifth grade teacher there enjoyed teaching a unit on the Holocaust and therefore had worked it into his curriculum. The question is what did he decide to eliminate from the curriculum because he wanted to teach the Holocaust unit? Having a curriculum map that identifies the units that are actually taught to compare with what is supposed to be taught will aid in finding similar situations like the Holocaust example.

CURRICULUM MAPPING—HORIZONTAL

A curriculum map is usually based on the calendar year and can simply be a list of what units are taught, when. This type of map, indicating the chronological order of when units are taught, is one way to determine the plan the teacher has for the school year.

FROM THE FIELD

One middle school teacher approached the teacher-librarian in September and said that she needed to reserve the library during the first week of April, for her eighth grade students to do research on the causes of the Civil War. The teacher knew she would need the library then, because she had a curriculum map or a list of when she planned to cover which topics.

In many instances a curriculum map provides additional information, including the subject matter of the unit, the skills being addressed, and the district and state standards that this unit supports (Jacobs 1997). A curriculum map with this complete information gives a visual account of what is happening in each individual classroom and how it is aligned to the required standards.

Curriculum mapping must not stop with the individual classroom, and as these individual maps are completed, they should be shared with other members of the faculty. In a middle school or secondary school, it is important that the same classes taught by different teachers present the same subject matter that supports the goals and objectives for that class. In an elementary school, it is important that each third grade teacher is covering the same information, so that the students acquire the skills that are intended for that grade level.

As the individual grade levels compare notes and make certain that what they are teaching is appropriate for their grade level, then a larger-picture view needs to occur, assessing the content across schools in the school district. This curriculum mapping process will provide individual teachers and district administrators with much-needed information about what actually is being taught and whether the students are receiving exposure to the district curriculum framework (Bishop 2007). It is an interesting experience to sit with a group of educators all teaching the same subject matter at the secondary level, or teaching the same grade level, and ask a specific question such as "Do the seventh graders all do a research paper?" The answers may be, "Yes, in my class they do," or "No, they don't; that is something they should accomplish in the eighth grade," or "Not this year because I ran out of time." A school district is responsible for the framework of the content presented to students during their school years. Curriculum mapping provides a picture of what is actually happening in each classroom in the district, allowing administrators and teachers to have a coordinated plan that will enhance the students' achievement level by providing a complete plan aligned with the district framework (Jacobs 2004).

CURRICULUM MAPPING—VERTICAL (SCOPE AND SEQUENCE)

After a curriculum map is constructed for each grade level and subject matter, then a vertical map, sometimes called a "scope and sequence," should be constructed to visually identify the standards, skills, and units that the student encounters during his or her time in the district. This K–12 map will illustrate the progress a student makes through the curriculum framework and the state and national standards. This map is a crucial tool in determining the educational journey of the student. Having this visual representation will illustrate any duplicate material that may be taught at different grade levels. For example, American history is typically taught in elementary school, middle school, and high school. Some students claim they have studied the early days of American history at each level and have not studied the history of the twentieth century. Having a vertical map (scope and sequence) will identify how in-depth a subject should be studied at each level. It will also provide the sequence of how skills should be presented.

What does this mean for the teacher-librarian? A curriculum map illustrates the content taught by the classroom teacher and the ways to present the materials needed to support the district and state standards. The teacher-librarian needs access to these maps to understand the subject matter that the students are learning. The purpose of the collection in the school library is to assist students and teachers with additional materials that support the information being presented in the classroom. To provide this support, the teacher-librarian can use the curriculum maps to determine materials needed that are available through the library collection. Developing a collection map will provide the teacher-librarian with this information.

INFORMATION SPECIALIST—COLLECTION MAPPING

While working with the teachers in curriculum mapping, the teacher-librarian should begin creating a collection map that has the same purpose as the curriculum map, except that it analyzes the materials in the library collection. A collection map shows what resources are in the collection, identified by the number of items in each Dewey section, and the map usually indicates the copyright date of the materials (Loertscher and Woolls 1999; Bishop 2007). This map is used to give a visual picture of each part of the collection. In the past, collection mapping was very time consuming, as the teacher-librarian would need to count the number of items in each Dewey section, determine the copyright date, and then develop a spreadsheet or chart that reflected this information. However, with the development of automated library systems, this process is now completed more efficiently. Most automated systems create reports identifying the number of items in a subject area with their corresponding copyright dates. The time needed for the teacher-librarian to gather this information is significantly reduced. When creating a collection map, the teacher-librarian should still examine each item to make certain it is in good condition, with covers intact and without missing or damaged pages (Franklin and Stephens 2009). The teacher-librarian should note the copyright date to make certain the material is still authentic and relevant for the collection. If possible, the newest edition of the book should be available for the students.

As the collection map is completed, the teacher-librarian should use this information to develop a collection development plan. The collection development plan assures that each part of the collection is evaluated in an organized manner to determine its relevance to the curriculum, its authenticity, and how up-to-date the items are. As noted earlier, the purpose of the school library collection is to support the elements of the curriculum being taught in the classrooms. Although items of general interest and on general topics should be included in the collection, the focus of the material in the collection should be to support the classroom content. In addition to supporting the curriculum, the teacher-librarian must include materials that support reading for learning and pleasure (AASL 2009). Using a collection map to analyze the library collection provides an accurate tool to acquire this information.

FROM THE FIELD

Sally, a teacher-librarian in an elementary school, organized a school-wide program based on the state award-winning children's books. She made certain that the library collection contained all of the books nominated for the state award. She then presented booktalks to the students each year in September when they returned to school. She continued marketing these books and using them for booktalks and readings throughout the year. In the spring, she organized the voting procedures. If the students had read three of the nominees, they could vote for their favorite selection. Because of Sally's dedication to making reading fun, most of the students had read more than the minimum of three. Sally also worked with the students to select good books for nominees for the following year. The students were engaged and enthused about this program. They caught Sally's enthusiasm and love of reading.

The tools of curriculum mapping and collection mapping provide the teacher-librarian with the information needed to practice his or her role as an information specialist. The teacher-librarian knows what materials are in the library collection through the collection map. He or she has a specific collection development plan that addresses how the resources will remain current. The teacher-librarian also knows what units are covered in the classrooms through the curriculum map and is therefore able to identify which materials to purchase for the collection. As an information specialist and a curriculum supporter, the teacher-librarian will make certain these purchased materials enhance the students' knowledge of the subject area. Having knowledge of the units in the classroom will assist the teacher-librarian in taking care of the students' informational needs.

INFORMATION SPECIALIST—ADDITIONAL CONSIDERATIONS

The teacher-librarian's responsibilities as information specialist extend to information resources in all types of formats, including electronic resources, Internet access, DVDs, e-books, and other items that either produce information or deliver information. The teacher-librarian must determine which items will be most effective in providing access to the needed information. This is an exciting process, as the teacher-librarian is on the cutting edge of learning how to use new electronic devices and evaluating them for their use and effectiveness in the library. This responsibility also includes being knowledgeable in the ethical use of these formats (AASL and AECT 1998; AASL 2009).

FROM THE FIELD

One elementary teacher-librarian saw the value of having the teachers learn how to use wikis for their own informational needs and to use with the students. The second graders in his school were completing research papers, and in order to have them share this information between classes, he had the second graders post their information on a wiki. He understood that by working with the students, the teachers would also learn how to use wikis. This accomplished his goal of implementing wikis as a viable information source for the students and staff (Howard 2008). By illustrating this relatively new technology, he was able to provide access to additional information for his students and their teachers.

Page (1999) explains three different curriculum roles for the teacher-librarian: curriculum implementation, addressing professional development programs for the teacher; curriculum enrichment, providing specific resources appropriate to the classroom; and curriculum support, which includes selection, acquisition, organization, and circulation of materials. The information specialist role for the teacher-librarian includes all of these aspects of accessing information: knowing the curriculum content in the classrooms; knowing the resources in the library, regardless of format; staying on the cutting edge of technology; and assisting the students and staff in learning how to use the appropriate technology for increased access to information. The teacher-librarian's curriculum responsibilities include these various functions.

INSTRUCTIONAL PARTNER

The previous discussion has centered on the curriculum role of the teacher-librarian in relationship to the content presented in the classroom. This curriculum role does not stop there. In fact, although being the information specialist is certainly necessary, unless that role extends to being an instructional partner through curriculum alignment, the teacher-librarian is not fulfilling his or her complete responsibility. The teacher-librarian needs to align his or her standards with the content standards of the teacher. Together, the two of them will be able to educate the whole child.

The teacher-librarian's curriculum includes multiple literacies (AASL 2007). *Information Power* (AASL and Association for Educational Communications and Technology 1998) presented the nine information literacy standards that teacher-librarians used to organize the school library curriculum, and in 2007, these standards were revised and the *Standards for the 21st-Century Learner* became the framework for the teacher-librarian's curriculum (AASL 2007). This framework includes four standards and the accompanying skills, dispositions in action, responsibilities, and self-assessment strategies. The new standards emphasize the necessity of reading as a skill for all types of information-gathering activities, including conducting research for learning and reading for personal enjoyment. These standards have expanded the definition of information literacy to embrace other types of literacy, including digital, visual, and technological. The crux of the new standards is that the students will use higher-level thinking skills to discover, evaluate, and create information that they can use as they become independent in the search for the knowledge they need as members of society. Having these standards to identify the skills students need to accomplish this, along with the students' responsibilities and questions for self-assessment, provides a roadmap the teacher-librarian will use to work with the students. These standards emphasize learning practices and the skills the student needs to continue the process of learning throughout life (AASL 2007).

The teachers have the content standards. The teacher-librarian has the *Standards for the 21st-Century Learner* (AASL 2007). The teacher's content standards involve facts and concepts contained in specific subject areas. The teacher-librarian's standards involve the process. For the student to fulfill his or her individual potential, there must be a marriage between these two types of standards. The students must understand the subject matter concepts and facts, and they must be able to understand the process of finding, synthesizing, evaluating, and creating the information they need to continue on the lifelong path of learning.

INSTRUCTIONAL PARTNER—CURRICULUM PLANNING

When *A Nation at Risk* (National Commission on Excellence in Education 1983) indicated that the state of American schools was a shambles, this opened the door to a variety of school reforms and school improvement practices (Danielson 2002; Harris 2005; Hughes-Hassell and Harada 2007). These reforms looked at the makeup of the school, the relationship of the teachers to the principals, the principal's role and management style, at shared decision making, accountability, and standards-based instruction, to name a few.

These school reform measures have impacted the role of the teacher in developing curriculum and working with the students. The current thinking supports the concept of constructivism that has the student taking an active part in his or her education (Loertscher 2000; Stripling 2003; Thomas 2004; Kuhlthau, Maniotes, and Caspari 2007). John Dewey (1916, 1938) supported this idea of constructivism and based his philosophy on the active engagement of students in their role as learners. The school has the responsibility to present the information, but the students must take the information and make it theirs through their own experiences and life situations. The students learn through doing and not through having facts presented for them to memorize. The learner must be engaged in the learning process (Sizer 1992; Kuhlthau 2004; Kuhlthau, Maniotes, and Caspari 2007). The teacher is expected to provide learning situations for the students; the teacher must learn how to redesign the curriculum in order to provide active experiences for the students. The instructional role of the teacher changes from sage-on-the-stage to the guide-on-the-side (Sizer 1992; Kuhlthau 1993; McKenzie 2000). At times, the teachers present facts that the students need to know; at other times, they are there to help the students figure out and discover on their own. The teacher can accomplish these two roles by implementing the process of inquiry into their lessons.

As seen earlier, the teacher-librarian's curriculum, the *Standards for the 21st-Century Learner* (AASL 2007), embraces inquiry as a framework for learning. This use of inquiry applies to the teacher-librarian as well as the classroom teacher. The teacher-librarian supports the students through learning activities that help them use the higher-level thinking skills, the critical thinking skills. If teacher-librarians are able to help the students think, to understand how to evaluate, synthesize, and create information, the students will be learners for their entire lives. In this age of information explosion, where the jobs that students will assume as adults have not been created and the technology that the students will use has also not been developed, the teacher-librarian must make certain the students are prepared with the necessary skills they need to harness the information they require throughout their lives. The trick is to take this opportunity provided through school reform and to align the *Standards for the 21st-Century Learner* (AASL 2007) with the teachers' content standards through this process of inquiry.

INSTRUCTIONAL PARTNER—INQUIRY-BASED LEARNING

Inquiry-based learning provides the teacher-librarian the opportunity to assist the students with their critical thinking skills. It is the process of assisting students with discovering in-depth information in order to answer the questions they have. Wiggins and McTighe (1998) describe it as the enduring understanding that encompasses the depth of knowledge the students need to make the information their own. It is an understanding that satisfies the students' questions concerning specific topics. The questions are answered not by the instructor telling the students the answer, but by the students taking an active role in determining the answer (Stripling 2003). Inquiry-based learning also narrows the focus of what is learned. Educators have been accused in the past of providing many facts about various topics and not providing the students with the in-depth exposure to important knowledge concepts (Zmuda, Kuklis, and Kline 2004).

Inquiry is not a curriculum; rather, it is a way of learning the content found in the curriculum (Kuhlthau, Maniotes, and Caspari 2007). It encompasses the process that is used to learn the subject area content required by the curriculum framework of the district and by state and national standards. The *Standards for the 21st-Century Learner* (AASL 2007) embraces this process of inquiry; therefore, the teacher-librarian is responsible for implementing this process by illustrating how students can find the information contained in the classroom content. Providing the foundation for inquiry-based lessons is an essential part of the curriculum role of the teacher-librarian. By aligning the inquiry process with the curriculum content from the classroom, the teacher-librarian will help the students assimilate the skills they will need for lifelong learning. In essence the students are learning how to think; they are using their higher-order thinking skills; they are becoming independent learners.

CURRICULUM RESPONSIBILITIES AT THE DISTRICT, STATE, AND NATIONAL LEVELS

The information presented in this chapter so far has focused on the teacher-librarian and his or her role at the school level. The teacher-librarian has a responsibility to continue this role throughout the learning community in the district and at the state level. As teachers review their curriculum at the district level, the teacher-librarian must play an active role in this process by joining the district curriculum revision commit-tees. Teachers at the school level will be familiar with the information and guidance the teacher-librarian has provided, and this will make the transition to the district com-mittee easier. Having the teacher-librarian's influence in the process of guided inquiry at the district level will be instrumental in the spread of this instructional content throughout the district.

State and national reforms in the curriculum area occur on a continual basis. As the teacher-librarian becomes adept at the district level, he or she must exert this influence at the state and national levels. This process can be facilitated through the state library association that is responsible for providing leadership at the state and the national levels. As teacher-librarians illustrate their expertise in the development of curriculum and show their willingness to provide leadership at the state and national levels, their goal of influencing the development of a guided inquiry curricu-lum aligned with the *Standards for the 21st-Century Learner* (AASL 2007) will be realized.

The teacher-librarian's role as information specialist and instructional partner at the school level is critical for the academic achievement of the students. This role extends to district, state, and national events. The teacher-librarian must be at the table in order for his or her influence to be felt.

LEADERSHIP REVISITED

The teacher-librarian understands what his or her responsibilities are regarding cur-riculum at the school, district, and national levels. The difficulty occurs with having the members of the learning community understand the extent of this role and how it has changed in recent years. In many places the image of the school librarian as the "keeper of the book" has been replaced with a truer picture of what the teacher-librarian's responsibilities are. But in some cases this outdated image remains. The teacher-librarian, by developing and exhibiting leadership skills, will reflect the true picture of the roles and responsibilities inherent in the position.

LEADERSHIP QUALITIES

A review of the literature shows that authors and researchers discuss a variety of skills necessary to exhibit leadership (Sheldon 1991; Lance, Rodney, and Hamilton-Pennell 2000; Schreiber and Shannon 2001; Kouzes and Posner 2002; Bennis 2003; Bennis and Nanus 2003; Marzano, Waters, and McNulty 2005; Woolls 2008). Synthesizing this leadership information and also analyzing the curriculum function, the teacher-librarian must develop the following skills: maintaining self-confidence, creating a vision, being a risk taker, remaining flexible, encouraging others, inspiring a sense of trust, developing communication skills through friendly interpersonal relationships, displaying personal passion, and exhibiting patience.

Kouzes and Posner (2002) provide a workable framework encompassing these qualities of leadership. Through their extensive research, they found that leaders must model the way, inspire a shared vision, challenge the process, enable others to act, and encourage the heart. Through example, the teacher-librarian shares his or her values of maintaining flexibility, developing trust, and inspiring enthusiasm and passion for using the curriculum to promote student achievement. Teacher-librarians have a vision of providing access to information that reflects, supports, and enhances the curriculum. They challenge the process through risk taking as they develop the curriculum partnership with teachers and explore the use of new technologies. As they work with teachers, they provide a safe environment of support for the collaborative partnership. And through the trust they develop with teachers, they encourage the heart, by valuing the contributions of each member of the curriculum team participating in the unit lesson. These five practices support the AASL (2009) vision for teacher-librarians in their leadership role.

LEADERSHIP SKILLS—INFORMATION SPECIALIST

The teacher-librarian, as the information specialist, may understand the process of curriculum mapping, but what leadership skills does he or she need in order to work with the teachers to obtain this information? This process is gradual, and the teacher-librarian must realize that much of his or her role depends on taking baby steps. The teacher-librarian must also assess the progress he or she has made as an information specialist. This reflection will instill in the teacher-librarian a feeling of self-confidence. These two qualities—patience and self-confidence—must be in the leadership treasure chest that the teacher-librarian develops; having these qualities will smooth the way when establishing the process of curriculum mapping with the teachers in the school.

The teacher-librarian must have confidence in his or her knowledge of the curriculum when approaching teachers to discuss the concept of curriculum mapping. The teacher-librarian understands the process of curriculum mapping and realizes that this can be a long and arduous process. Instead of trying to institute the entire process right away, the initial conversation may be asking the teachers in an informal setting what units they teach during each month or semester of the year. The teacher-librarian can keep track of this information without causing the teachers any extra work. In some schools the teacher-librarian may be able to accumulate this information only by progressing through one year, keeping track of what units are taught, when.

The very first day on the job, the teacher-librarian must use his or her interpersonal skills to show the members of the school community the type of personality he or she has. One should be warm, friendly, humorous, accepting, and welcoming. The teacher-librarian will develop deep and trusting relationships through these interpersonal skills. As a result, when the teacher-librarian approaches a teacher to begin the process of curriculum mapping, this self-confidence and warm, friendly personality will provide a substantial infrastructure for success.

FROM THE FIELD

Jackie, a teacher-librarian, knew that the new language arts curriculum would be quite different from the one currently being used in the school. She made certain that she received a copy of the textbooks for the library and then reviewed the support materials at the end of each chapter. In a systematic way, she charted which support materials were part of the existing library collection. She also prepared an order to obtain items that she knew would be in high demand. Using her initiative and vision of aligning the new curriculum with the library collection, she became prepared for approaching the teachers as they implemented the new curriculum.

As the teacher-librarian creates the collection map and a collection development plan, it is helpful to reflect upon the reason for spending time aligning the collection with the curriculum. The vision of the teacher-librarian should be one of seamless access for the members of the learning community to the information they need to continue on their journey of acquiring information. Bennis and Nanus (2003) encourage leaders to have an agenda for accomplishing their goals. This agenda provides a focus or a vision of what the leaders will accomplish. Teacher-librarians as they are creating this collection development plan will be providing for this seamless access to information.

LEADERSHIP SKILLS—INSTRUCTIONAL PARTNER

Risk taking is the process of exposing oneself to creating something new. It is being comfortable and unafraid when considering a new way that challenges the existing processes for accomplishing the daily routine. Kouzes and Posner (2002) call this challenging the process. Leaders must look at what is being done and then reflect on what needs to change to improve the existing practice. Teachers may not understand the importance of the teacher-librarian aligning the multitude of literacies with the standards through content-based inquiry lessons. The teacher-librarian must challenge the process and becomes a risk taker as he or she works with the teachers in implementing these inquiry lessons.

FROM THE FIELD

Molly understands the value of providing leadership in the area of curriculum. Molly gradually established herself as an effective leader with the teachers at her K–5 school. Developing this sense of trust with the staff did not occur on the first day she was hired; rather, it was a gradual process of letting the teachers get to know her and see how passionate she was about her responsibilities of providing access to information as an information specialist and an instructional partner. One method she used was through implementing a grade level program. After attending a workshop discussing grade level curriculum, Molly approached her four third grade teachers with the idea of having a project that would engage the students and address specific content and information literacy standards. Upon Molly's suggestion, the group wholeheartedly supported the theme of the Iditarod Dog Sled Race. This unit addressed language arts, social studies, geography, and science, as well as the Educational Technology and Information Literacy standards. The activities included having the students select a musher and research the musher's life, which was then illustrated on poster board; daily tracking of the musher's progress; daily comparison of the weather in the school's location with that in Nome, Alaska; making literature connections in the library and the classroom; and conducting research on the history of the Iditarod. Although the project was specifically designed for the third grade, Molly and the teachers developed activities that included the entire school and the community. Each third grade student wore a badge with his or her musher's picture on it. The teachers and other members of the staff were encouraged to ask the students about their mushers and the mushers' progress. The students were responsible for answering these impromptu questions. A large map was displayed in a prominent place in the school, and each student tracked the progress of his or her musher by moving a musher-like form on the route of the Iditarod.

Molly developed the community connection through the local mushers' group, who visited the school prior to the Iditarod, bringing with them their equipment and dogs. The mushers gave demonstrations on how the equipment worked, and the students enjoyed this and getting to know the members of the dog teams. Students were given an opportunity to participate in the "I-Did-A-Read" contest by writing persuasive essays indicating why they should have an opportunity to pet the dogs. The winners of the contest were allowed to actually pet the dogs.

This grade level project was a complete success. The teachers and teacher-librarian developed a unit that supported the tenets of inquiry through engaging the students in constructivist activities. The unit planners organized the activities around exposure to the various content and the *Standards for the 21st-Century Learner* (2007). The Iditarod unit was an event that the students remember long past their elementary school days.

Molly exhibited the leadership qualities necessary for a curriculum leader through this unit. She was a risk taker when she first approached the teachers concerning the unit. The trust she had built with the teachers and her self-confidence in knowing the curriculum provided her with courage to begin this process. Her vision for such activities to support access to information and her passion for working with the students were evident in this process. This example illustrates leadership at its best.

CONCLUSION

The teacher-librarian's responsibility in the area of curriculum at the school level involves two roles: information specialist and instructional partner. The teacher-librarian, as an information specialist, must know what the national, state, and district standards are for the classroom content. Along with having knowledge of the standards, the teacher-librarian should be familiar with the textbooks used in the classroom and the best practices used in the district. Many school districts are engaged in specific school reforms, and the teacher-librarian must have knowledge of these reforms and how they are implemented in the district. If specific instructional processes are supported by the district, the teacher-librarian should be aware of and understand these processes. In addition to understanding the required curriculum, the teacher-librarian must be aware of the manner in which the curriculum is being presented in the classroom. Curriculum mapping is a tool that will provide this information. Along with being aware of the content that is being presented in the classroom, the teacher-librarian needs to create a collection map that identifies the materials in the library collection. By comparing the curriculum maps and the collection map, the teacher-librarian will be able to determine what sources need to be purchased to support the teachers' curriculum.

The second area of responsibility for the teacher-librarian, as an instructional partner, is aligning the *Standards for the 21st-Century Learner* (AASL 2007) and the classroom content. In order to accomplish this, the teacher-librarian must know the standards, understand higher-level critical thinking skills, and have grasped the process of guided inquiry learning. The teacher-librarian will then be able to develop inquiry lessons with the teachers to make certain the students become lifelong learners.

To fulfill these roles the teacher-librarian must be a leader. The leadership qualities that will assist in the curriculum role are patience, flexibility, and self-confidence, as well as being able to inspire a sense of trust; being a risk taker; having and sharing a vision; encouraging others; developing communication skills through a friendly, accepting personality; and working with enthusiasm and passion. Becoming a leader and exhibiting leadership qualities in the curriculum area is a necessary requirement for fulfilling the role of the teacher-librarian as an information specialist and instructional partner.

REFERENCES

American Association of School Librarians (AASL). 2007. *Standards for the 21st-century learner*. Chicago: American Library Association. http://www.ala.org/aasl/standards.
———. 2009. *Empowering learners: Guidelines for school library media programs*. Chicago: American Association of School Librarians.
American Association of School Librarians (AASL) and Association for Educational Communications and Technology. 1988. *Information Power: Guidelines for school library media programs*. Chicago: American Library Association.
———. 1998. *Information power: Building partnerships for learning*. Chicago: American Library Association.
Bennis, W. 2003. *On becoming a leader*. New York: Basic books.
Bennis, W., and B. Nanus. 2003. *Leaders: Strategies for taking charge* (2nd ed.). New York: HarperBusiness Essentials.
Bishop, K. 2007. *The collection program in schools: Concepts, practices, and information sources* (4th ed.). Westport, CT: Libraries Unlimited.
Craver, K. W. 1986. The changing instructional role of the high school library media specialist, 1950–1984: A survey of professional literature, standards, and research studies. *School Library Media Quarterly* 14 (4): 183–191.
Danielson, C. 2002. *Enhancing student achievement: A framework for school improvement*. Alexandria, VA: Association for Supervision and Curriculum Development.

Dewey, J. 1916. *Democracy and education: An introduction to the philosophy of education.* Sioux Falls, SD: NuVision Publishing, LLC.

———. 1938. *Experience and education.* New York: Collier Books.

Eisenberg, M. B., and R. E. Berkowitz. 1988. *Curriculum initiative: An agenda and strategy for library media programs.* Norwood, NJ: Ablex Publishing Corporation.

Elmore, R. F. 2000. *Building a new structure for school leadership.* Washington, DC: Albert Shanker Institute.

Franklin, P., and C. G. Stephens. 2009. Use standards to draw curriculum maps. *School Library Media Activities Monthly* 25 (9): 44–45.

Harris, E. L. 2005. *Key strategies to improve schools: How to apply them contextually.* Lanham, MD: Rowman and Littlefield Education.

Hartzell, G. N. 2001. The implications of selected school reform approaches for school library media services. *School Library Media Research Quarterly* 4. http://www.ala.org/ala/mgrps/divs/aasl/aaslpubsandjournals/slmrb/slmrcontents/volume42001/hartzell.cfm (accessed April 18, 2009).

Harvey, C. A. 2008. *No school library left behind: Leadership, school improvement and the media specialist.* Columbus, OH: Linworth Publishing.

Howard, J. K. 2008. The relationship between school culture and an effective school library program: Four case studies. Abstract in *Dissertation Abstracts International* 70 (02). Publication No.: AAT 3347462.

Howard, J. K., and S. A. Eckhardt. 2005. Why action research? the leadership role of the library media specialist. *Library Media Connection* 24 (2): 32–34.

Hughes-Hassell, S., and V. H. Harada, eds. 2007. *School reform and the school library media specialist.* Westport, CT: Libraries Unlimited.

Jacobs, H. H. 1997. *Mapping the big picture: Integrating curriculum and assessment K–12.* Alexandria, VA: Association for Supervision and Curriculum Development.

———, ed. 2004. *Getting results with curriculum mapping.* Alexandria, VA: Association for Supervision and Curriculum Development.

Kester, D. D., and A. J. Plummer. 2004. Francis Henne and the development of school library standards. *Library Trends* 52 (4): 952–962.

Kouzes, J. M., and B. Z. Posner. 2002. *The leadership challenge* (3rd ed.). San Francisco: Jossey-Bass.

Kuhlthau, C. C. 1993. Implementing a process approach to information skills: A study identifying indicators of success in library media programs. *School Library Media Quarterly* 22 (1). http://www.ala.org/ala/mgrps/divs/aasl/aaslpubsandjournals/slmrb/editorschoiceb/infopower/selectkuhlthau1.cfm (accessed March 30, 2009).

———. 2004. *Seeking meaning: A process approach to library and information services* (2nd ed.). Westport: CT: Libraries Unlimited.

Kuhlthau, C. C., L. K. Maniotes, and A. K. Caspari. 2007. *Guided inquiry: Learning in the 21st century.* Westport, CT: Libraries Unlimited.

Lance, K. C., M. J. Rodney, and C. Hamilton-Pennell. 2000. *How school librarians help kids achieve standards: The second Colorado study.* San Jose, CA: Hi Willow Research and Publishing.

Loertscher, D. V. 2000. *Taxonomies of the school library media program* (2nd ed.). San Jose, CA: Hi Willow Research and Publishing.

Loertscher, D. V., and B. Woolls. 1999. *Building a school library collection plan: A beginning handbook with Internet assist.* San Jose, CA: Hi Willow Research and Publishing.

Marzano, R. J., T. Waters, and B. A. McNulty. 2005. *School leadership that works: From research to results.* Alexandria, VA: Association for Supervision and Curriculum Development.

McKenzie, J. 2000. *Beyond technology: Questioning, research and the information literate school.* Bellingham, WA: FNO Press.

National Commission on Excellence in Education. 1983. *A nation at risk.* Washington, DC: U.S. Department of Education.

Oberg, A. 1999. The school librarian and the classroom teacher: Partners in curriculum planning. In *Foundations for effective school library media programs,* ed. K. Haycock, 167–173. Greenwood Village, CO: Libraries Unlimited.

Page, C. 1999. Information skills in the curriculum: Developing a school-based curriculum. In *Foundations for effective school library media programs,* ed. K. Haycock, 122–129. Greenwood Village, CO: Libraries Unlimited.

Pickard, P. W. 1993. Current research: The instructional consultant role of the school library media specialist. *School Library Media Quarterly* 21 (3): 115–122.

Schmoker, M. 2006. *Results now: How we can achieve unprecedented improvement in teaching and learning.* Alexandria, VA: Association for Supervision and Curriculum Development.

Schreiber, B., and J. Shannon. 2001. Developing library leaders for the 21st century. In *Leadership in the library and information science professions: Theory and practice,* ed. M. D. Winston, 35–60. New York: Haworth Press, Inc. Co-published simultaneously as *Journal of Library Administration* 32 (3/4).

Sheldon, B. E. 1991. *Leaders in libraries: Styles and strategies for success.* Chicago: American Library Association.

Sizer, T. R. 1992. *Horace's school: Redesigning the American high school.* Boston: Houghton Mifflin Company.

Spillane, J. P., R. Halverson, and J. B. Diamond. 2004. Towards a theory of leadership practice: A distributed perspective. *Journal of Curriculum Studies* 36 (1): 3–34.

Stripling, B. K. 2003. Inquiry-based learning. In *Curriculum connections through the library,* eds. B. K. Stripling and S. Hughes-Hassell, 1–39. Westport, CT: Libraries Unlimited.

Thomas, N. P. 2004. *Information literacy and information skills instruction: Applying research to practice in the school library media center* (2nd ed.). Westport, CT: Libraries Unlimited.

Turner, P. M., and A. M. Riedling. 2003. *Helping teachers teach: A school library media specialist's role* (3rd ed.). Westport, CT: Libraries Unlimited.

Wiggins, G., and J. McTighe. 1998. *Understanding by design.* Columbus, OH: Merrill Prentice Hall.

Wolcott, L. L. 1994. Understanding how teachers plan: Strategies for successful instructional partnerships. *School Library Media Quarterly* 22 (3). http://www.ala.org/ala/mgrps/divs/aasl/aaslpubsandjournals/slmrb/editorschoiceb/infopower/selectwolcott.cfm (accessed March 30, 2009).

Woolls, B. 1990. When leadership is followership: Comparing practice and theory in library education for children's and school librarians. In *Library education and leadership: Essays in honor of Jane Ann Hannigan,* eds. S. S. Inter and K. E. Vandergrift, 195–207. Metuchen, NJ: Scarecrow Press.

———. 2008. *The school library media manager* (4th ed.). Westport, CT: Libraries Unlimited.

Zmuda, A., and V. Harada. 2008. *Librarians as learning specialists.* Westport CT: Libraries Unlimited.

Zmuda, A., R. Kuklis, and E. Kline. 2004. *Transforming schools: Creating a culture of continuous improvement.* Alexandria, VA: Association for Supervision and Curriculum Development.

Zweizig, D. L., and D. M. Hopkins. 1999. *Lessons from Library Power enriching teaching and learning: Final report of the evaluation of the National Library Power Initiative.* Englewood, CO: Libraries Unlimited.

7

Pride and Prejudice
and Technology Leadership

Kristin Fontichiaro

PROLOGUE

The mantle that comes with the word "leader" is a heavy one. It can be difficult for school library media specialists (SLMSs) to wrap their heads around the concept of leadership. After all, most SLMSs have little to no formal authority, yet they are often entrusted with the largest discretionary budget in a school building. They are not administrators, yet they can have profound impact on instructional practices. Most have completed significant additional coursework beyond that required for a teaching certificate, yet they are the peers of their classroom colleagues.

Technology leadership is a particularly multifaceted challenge, wrapping into it instruction, collaborative practices, hardware, and software. Technology hardware is expensive, a very public expenditure. As a result, missteps or bobbles in decision making are expensive and can draw more attention than other acquisitions. For its perception as a pile of wires and switches, technology arouses strong emotions among those who use it and who build and safeguard their networks. Often, it places SLMSs in the middle of a tug-of-war between the needs and wants of administration, the technical services department, and the needs and user preferences of building staff and students. Technology integration is also a challenge, as educational institutions have a responsibility not only to teach how to navigate a particular piece of hardware or software but also how to use it to serve the larger purpose of student learning and content understanding. But despite these many challenges, we should be honest; it is fun.

But what does it mean to be a technology leader? When I pause to answer this question, my mind leaps to a scene in the British television miniseries *Lost in Austen*, which chronicles the time travel of Amanda Price from twenty-first-century London back into the days of *Pride and Prejudice*.

In one scene, Miss Price and several middle-class women are riding in a carriage. When the carriage loses a wheel, the time-traveling heroine wonders why no one is taking any action. The groom, who does not know how to ride a horse, begins walking away to get help. As a result, it will be some time before they are rescued. The other women do nothing, because it would not be proper for a Georgian lady to ride one of the carriage horses without a saddle, much less repair a carriage. And so they sit for some time.

As I watched this video a few months ago, the thought popped into my head that had there been an SLMS on board, he or she would have hopped out of the carriage, brandished a book tape, a USB cord, and three half-chewed pencils; rigged a repair; hopped into the driver's seat; and driven on. On some level, that is technology leadership in the proverbial nutshell: doing whatever it takes, from envisioning a technology overhaul to crawling under a computer table to fix a loose connection to empowering students to learn to their maximum potential.

MY PERSPECTIVE

I am a practicing elementary SLMS in an upper middle-class district (though, at the time of this essay's writing, that future was clouded by the bankruptcy of two of the area's major employers: Chrysler and General Motors). As a result, we receive more per-pupil funding than many surrounding districts and have budgets that allow more resources and more staff for our students. Our students and teachers come from technology-rich households. Most have high-speed Internet connections and cable television. High-tech homes mean that even our youngest students hit the ground running with technology. Several students report that they make PowerPoint presentations at home for fun. One regularly brings a personal digital camcorder to school. Some have playdates to create stop-motion animation or film videos. Several have iPods. In four years, I have had only one kindergartener who did not intuitively know how to use a computer mouse upon arrival. We have half-time in-house technical support, with someone whose focus is solely on technology troubleshooting and upgrades. A small, neighborhood school within a stable community, we have remarkably low turnover in enrollment. Daily attendance is high, and many parents are deeply engaged in their children's school. And so my journey toward leadership may be quite different from that of other SLMSs who face greater socioeconomic challenges. I admit this bias up front and beg the reader's indulgence in understanding that I can speak only from my own experiences.

CHANGING THE PARADIGM

Here is the joyful core of technology leadership: deciding on an adventure, envisioning it, and then empowering others to see and share that vision. It is the joy of discovering how new technology tools can solve existing problems or excite teachers and students into new ways of learning and demonstrating understanding. It is emailing colleagues from a tech conference because you cannot wait the few hours that might pass before you see them—what you have just learned is *that* exciting. It is the pleasure of discovering, side by side with staff or students, a new tool or a new way of doing things. And those pleasures come when SLMSs are willing to shift their outlook.

In past years, when computers were constrained to computer labs or media centers and few had Internet access or even computers at home, it was easy for the SLMS to perceive him- or herself as the competent keeper of, and trainer about, "the equipment." Generally, the SLMS would be trained first and then pass on that training to the staff in the building. Professional development may have consisted of getting teachers to use and master preselected tools. Technology was relatively static and "masterable," though poor dial-up connections or corrupted floppy disks were common culprits. Success depended on being able to execute the proper series of keystrokes so that the desired result would occur.

Acquired at great financial cost, hardware and software tools were likely to be used for years. As a result, getting teachers to adopt those tools was of great importance. SLMSs felt they had to "master" a new piece of hardware or software before sharing it with students or staff, making themselves a mediator between user and tool. Many SLMSs felt like pioneers in this era, and their confidence was built on the sense that they could achieve and then maintain a working knowledge of one piece of software at a time.

Over time, the cost of purchasing computer equipment and high-speed Internet access has dropped considerably, making their acquisition a reality for more and more households. My black-and-white Apple ImageWriter II dot matrix printer cost a whopping $416 in the early 1990s, whereas my 2008 color laser printer cost about $150, and my Macintosh Classic that cost $1100 when I entered college in 1991 had a fraction of the computing power of my iPhone. With the influx of technology in homes, that once-firmly established pecking order of SLMS-to-teacher-to-student began to change. Teachers began coming to the SLMS having heard about tools or having tried them on their own. The proliferation of Web-based information and free online, shareware, and open source programs knocked that paradigm off of its pedestal. The number of possible hardware and software configurations became exponential, and "mastery" of a software bundle was no longer practical. Instead, SLMSs now flourish as jacks-of-all-trades, familiar with a wide range of tools but perhaps not exploring any one tool in depth until the need arises.

The students have changed as well. They are no longer passively waiting for the teacher to introduce a new tool. They now come, as do my students described earlier, with much greater prior knowledge and sometimes with informally gained expertise on technology operations. Technology information no longer flows in a linear path from the technical services department to media specialists to teachers and finally to students. Now, the playing field has been leveled; the formal hierarchy has collapsed.

One of the great joys of working with the teachers in my school has been watching adults relax and allow students to teach students or for staff to learn from one another. While I am still relied upon as someone who scours journals, Twitter, the blogosphere, and more for the latest tools, I am not alone. I am not driving the bus anymore; we all take turns.

It takes courage to say, "It's okay if we share in the learning" and to share in the sense of discovery with staff and students. When a staff member asks for help with a new tool that I do not know, I have learned to ask, "Would you like me to learn it in advance and then teach you, or would you like to learn side by side?" Imagine my surprise to discover that some staff members actually *prefer* that we learn simultaneously! What a relief that I do not have to be The Expert. We can become experts together, celebrating one another's findings and "aha!" moments.

Similarly, the traditional technology model is for the SLMS or classroom teacher to model step-by-step instructions on how to use a tool or piece of software. But in today's world, many students know how to use these tools already. Having the courage to step aside and let children teach children is awkward at first and awakens internal worries: "Aren't I supposed to be doing the teaching?" But soon, that worry is replaced with a sense of relief: "Wow! Now that they are teaching each other how to make slide transitions, I am free to focus on their cognitive processes, synthesis, and self-reflection."

This shift in pedagogical focus is evident in the 2007 refreshed *National Educational Technology Standards for Students* (NETS*S), published by the International Society for Technology in Education (2007). The NETS*S set forth a technology integration plan that shifts the focus away from understanding the parts of a computer or what to click in Microsoft Excel. Instead, there are six NETS*S facets that show how technology should be used to foster different modalities of learning, build student-centered learning communities, conduct and show findings from research, encourage creative thinking and problem solving, and use technology in ethical ways (International Society for Technology in Education 2007). The values articulated in the refreshed NETS*S map perfectly to the American Association for School Librarians' (AASL) *Standards for the 21st-Century Learner*, also released in 2007 (AASL 2007).

These new visioning documents clarify that it is no longer enough to have elementary children use a mouse to digitally draw with a drawing program, because that limits their interaction to the operations level. It is no longer enough to evaluate students based solely on their ability to insert graphics or transitions into a PowerPoint slide show. Those are no longer challenging objectives for students. The challenge is how to make sense of boundless data and information and share that understanding with others. Now teachers can put their focus on *how* that tool is being used, and SLMSs can be part of that shift.

Leadership does not require that we be the conduit between the user and the tool. Leadership can be the willingness to let others share in or take turns leading the journey instead of insisting that we always pave the way first. Serendipity can occur when colleagues learn together. Classroom teachers and the SLMSs can see the same tool or resource through different eyes, and we not only learn the tool together, but together, we brainstorm uses for the tool, and I discover new avenues I had not previously considered. Leadership does not mean we are the gatekeepers to the tech kingdom; it is reveling in the camaraderie of shared ownership.

KEEPING UP

Levitov (2007) identifies five roles for the SLMS: professional learner, visionary, leader, connector, and teacher. SLMSs who see their work as a profession, not "a job," know that they must continue to seek new knowledge and best practice. Recognizing professional learning as an ongoing core job function means embracing persistence as a lifelong habit and one's career as an ongoing journey.

Persistence is also essential when working with teachers, especially those who are reluctant to move forward with technology. They may feel more secure remembering the past instead of looking at the future. Often, our administrators entrust us with moving these colleagues forward. With reluctant technology adopters, progress tends to come in baby steps, not leaps. Embracing the persistence model means that we are "in it for the long haul" and will not give up if the first, second, or third effort fails. Patiently, we recognize that if we stay calm and focused on the end result, we sustain the energy needed to continue to nudge colleagues forward (Fontichiaro 2009), recognizing and celebrating small victories.

The Japanese have a term in industrial practice for this outcome: *kaizen*, a term generally translated to mean continuous improvement. What is education, if not the process of continuous improvement for students? SLMSs have a responsibility to mentor colleagues and model for students what continuous improvement looks like. There are many paths to continuous improvement, including the following:

- **Membership in state, national, and/or international library and technology associations.** These memberships often include a print journal as well as online resources such as blogs, wikis, listservs, or community groups developed with social tools such as Facebook, Ning, or Twitter.
- **Professional reading in library journals, educational technology magazines, blogs, and Twitter feeds.** Being well-read in library literature such as the American Association for School Librarians' *Knowledge Quest*, or the independent publications *School Library Monthly*, *Library Media Connection*, *School Library Journal*, and *Teacher Librarian*, is important, but so is reading *outside* and *beyond* library literature. For example, the science field writes vigorously about pursuing inquiry (a value also held by librarians), and their writing offers a new perspective to our work in libraries. A blog such as Joyce Valenza's NeverEndingSearch (http://www.slj.com) or Buffy Hamilton's The Unquiet Librarian (http://theunquietlibrarian .wordpress.com) gives terrific insights about new technology tools and resources to help students engage with library resources, while a non-library blog like that written by David Pogue, Pogue's Posts (http://pogue.blogs.nytimes.com/), keeps librarians attuned with popular consumer electronics and technology trends. For great educational technology Twitter feeds (microblogs where each post is limited to 140 characters), try Will Richardson (http://www .twitter.com/willrich45), Steve Dembo (http://www.twitter.com/teach42), or David Warlick (http://www.twitter.com/dwarlick).
- **Attendance at face-to-face professional development workshops or conferences.** The traditional sit-and-get workshops of the past are becoming hands on. Wireless connectivity means an empty room can become a computer lab in minutes, as participants unpack laptops from their conference totes. Hands-on workshops give SLMSs a terrific opportunity to learn about new tools and strategies and kick the tires. Come Monday morning, they have something new to share with staff. Face-to-face conferences offer terrific networking opportunities, too (Harvey 2009).
- **Virtual professional development.** If taking time away from work or family for a conference is not possible, consider learning virtually. Learn how to use a Web 2.0 tool via a YouTube video. Create a virtual persona and head over to the professional development site housed by the International Society for Technology in Education in Second Life (International Society for Technology in Education, "ISTE Second Life") for free interactions with national leaders. Participate in self-paced professional development based on Helene Blowers's Learning 2.0 project for the Public Library of Charlotte and Mecklenburg County (also known as the 23 Things project) (Blowers 2006). Sign on to your association's listserv. Monitor the conference Web sites, where posting video, audio, or copies of handouts, even for non-attendees, is becoming the norm. (One great site is http://www.fetc.org/.)
- **Local networking.** Never doubt the power of a pizza to get new ideas flowing. Every technology leader needs a cadre of colleagues who can meet after school, hop onto Wi-Fi, and brainstorm. In some cases, this cadre comes from building or media colleagues; in others, it may require seeking colleagues from the public library or business world. Additional colleagues will appear as you reach out into national conferences, but the truth is, sometimes you need to be looking at the same screen.

- **Parents.** Some high-tech parents with flexible daytime schedules would love to come in and help you, your staff, and students use new equipment or software. But working parents can help, too. They often use some of the same tools used in schools. While volunteering during the work day can be difficult, some are eager to pitch in if they can evaluate tools, software, or Web sites after work.
- **Experimenting.** These days, one is more likely to get a computer virus than to wreck a computer from making a mistake. Go ahead! Take a new tool or software for a whirl! Open source software (such as Audacity for podcasting, http://audacity.sourceforge.net, or OpenOffice, a free, open source suite similar to the Microsoft Office package, available at http://openoffice.org) costs nothing to try. Many high-end software packages, such as Microsoft Office or Adobe products, are available for 30-day trials. And many Web sites for creating blogs, wikis, digital posters, slide shows, captioned photos, and more are free!

Engaging in ongoing learning can sound like a challenge. Start small: attend a single conference, or fire up Google Reader or Bloglines as easy online RSS readers to manage the blogs you like. *Kaizen* does not require an about-face or revolution. Gradual baby steps are okay *if* you commit to one after another. Rather than pitching out old practices, think about making changes that keep the best of what has been happening in your school library and refining from there. *Kaizen* is not always about swapping out one practice for another. It can also be about improving what is already successful, like polishing a diamond (Economist.com, 2009). Persistence is the staying-power that lets us polish that diamond. It helps the SLMS see new challenges as polishing opportunities, not as negative drags on one's energy. Do not resign yourself to the status quo; keep moving.

GATHERING DIVERSE PERSPECTIVES

A single perspective, coupled with pride, can be the Achilles' heel of a library media specialist. The diverse ecosystem of student and staff needs means that a successful SLMS cannot make decisions alone, as in a vacuum. Technology leadership means gathering feedback and input in multiple ways: formal and informal, observed and discussed.

Observation can be a powerful way to gather feedback, as SLMSs have a unique global perspective on how technology is being used. By observing computer lab activities and technology use in media centers, they can see trends that span across grade levels and classroom divides. They can identify effective practices ("Hands in your lap when I'm talking in the lab") and ineffective ones ("Just fill in the template and you're done"). They are able to observe, for example, that multiple teachers are engaging students in eerily similar projects ("Why are so many grades doing PowerPoint projects about the 50 states?"). They are often the first to observe an increase in students working with technology without teacher intervention or to discover high school students using a proxy site to access blocked content. All of these observations can inform the need to celebrate growth, revisit policy, rethink the types of technology mini-lessons students need, consider additional subscriptions or hardware acquisitions, or update professional development offerings.

Information can be collected from the school's mission statement and district curriculum. Knowing the school's values and vision for successful students as reflected in the mission statement is the starting point for great program design (Zmuda 2007), which leads to better lesson planning with colleagues. Ask colleagues how they see the school library and the SLMS as meeting the mission and the curriculum. Some SLMSs carry this out by convening technology committees, sending emails, hosting online surveys, or opening a discussion in the teachers' lounge.

Leadership means some tough decisions will come along with that increased input. For example, if many teachers request a tool, does that mean the SLMS is obligated to purchase it, even if it does not meet district curriculum or tech network standards? Be sure to consider this in advance and structure the requests for input so that teachers do not interpret your requests for information as a blank check! Unfortunately, teachers tend to manage only very small materials budgets for their classrooms and often do not have experience with book fair fundraisers, district versus building funds, or acquisition policies. They may not realize the size of or restrictions placed upon your budget. In that situation, consider structuring queries carefully so as not to dash false hopes. Have grant proposals at the ready and offer to co-apply if teachers' desires exceed existing finances.

Another way to gather information is through staff and committee meetings. These are additional opportunities to identify areas where technology can support administrative tasks, collaboration, teaching, and learning. For example, consider the arduous tasks of school accreditation, a laborious multi-year process. A school improvement team could benefit from online project management tools, Web-based surveys to gather and process data, collective access to the same server folder, collaborative authoring tools such as wikis or Google Docs, or podcast or video interviews. In the previous accreditation cycle, many of these tasks would have been done by hand, and staff may not realize that automation tools exist. The SLMS can also help by setting up these tools, thus saving valuable staff time.

Similarly, meetings can identify opportunities to use free or inexpensive tools to replace processes that were once costly. For example, a school facing a budget crisis might benefit from publishing a blog instead of a printed weekly newsletter, which would save on paper costs. A school district that can no longer afford cable access in order to broadcast school board meetings might be able to stream them for free with Ustream.tv. A district that cannot afford to buy a software upgrade might benefit from a free or low-cost Web-based alternative.

Meetings can also identify instructional weaknesses that could be ameliorated with technology resources. A math department struggling to teach types of graphs to elementary students might benefit from a Web-based tutorial. A music teacher may wish to offer composition opportunities to advanced students, and the SLMS can point them toward a myriad of resources, from free audio loops to downloadable graph paper to free or low-cost composition software. All of these scenarios represent cases where the staff recognizes a need but may not realize that a technology-based solution exists.

Of course, sometimes the reverse happens: teachers demand a particular tool. For example, a teacher in my building wanted to acquire Tom Snyder's Timeliner program, for which a building license would cost a whopping $1500, more than twice our annual software budget! It seemed steep for a single lesson. I asked how she wanted to use the tool and, knowing what features were important to her, explored online and found Free-Timeline (http://www.free-timeline.com/timeline.jsp). It turned out that the free site met her objectives, freeing up our tight budget to purchase something else. (Since then, a new free multimedia timeline maker, XTimeline, has become available: http://www.xtimeline.com.) Similarly, when we began podcasting, we looked at expensive podcasting software and thought implementation was out of our price range. When we discovered Audacity for free (http://audacity.sourceforge.net), podcasting could blossom because the software could be pushed out to every computer. Just as a reference interview proceeds so that the librarian can clarify the patron need and meet it appropriately, consider technology requests as a similar opportunity. What is really needed? A tool, or *that* tool?

In gathering data, do not forget your own expertise. Consider your own experiences and instincts. Your accumulated expertise will help you decide whether you should buy inexpensive (flimsy) headphones or fewer high-quality pairs, just as you decide whether you should buy paperbacks or hardcover books.

QUESTIONING

Today's SLMSs know that asking thoughtful questions is one pathway to deeper understanding in their students. Questioning leads to learning. This is true for both adults and children. SLMSs have special resource evaluation skills that can aid in decision making. It may be tempting to unquestioningly follow every technology trend or decision, but those who simply embrace everything that comes down the pike, without having a strong pedagogical foundation that connects those trends to instructional goals, may find reduced support from classroom colleagues.

Technology leadership is not about blind admiration or worshiping technology or newness. Students do not benefit from sycophantic, unquestioning support. SLMSs can show leadership by questioning how a tool might be used, what potential problems could arise, and whether the benefits outweigh the concerns.

For example, podcasting is a wonderful way to awaken a sense of voice and theatricality in students (Fontichiaro 2008b). The SLMS can pave the way by evaluating potential bandwidth issues, reflecting on potential classroom integration, considering which students might benefit most, considering whether to buy a single high-end license or use the free and open source software Audacity, and deciding whether to buy a few expensive but more durable headsets or amass a huge quantity of inexpensive, less robust ones. Addressing these questions in advance minimizes implementation challenges later.

As a secondary example, what about hosting teens in Second Life? It sounds wonderfully progressive and motivating, but are there concerns that the acceptable use policy needs revision? Who monitors after-hours access? What potential benefits are there? Can the infrastructure handle the bandwidth needs? For elementary schools, should money and time be spent developing students' keyboarding skills? That is a pragmatic question as mobile devices become more popular. Only through questioning the benefits versus the costs at media meetings, at staff meetings, and in informal conversations can a confident decision be reached.

Questioning leads to more thoughtful decision making. "What if we ____?" "What would change if ____?" or, "What is the best/worst thing that could happen if ____?" are all typical questions that might arise. In asking such questions, the SLMS models inquiry and curiosity, which brings the AASL *Standards for the 21st-Century Learner* to life. And as a result, schools spend less money on untested "wonder products" and instead focus more time on using those tools effectively with students.

Healthy skepticism is an asset for the SLMS. Merely embracing everything because it is new belies the collection development expertise of the SLMS. Making wise and strategic choices is part of the job of the librarian. If a tool or resource does not improve teaching and learning, do not use it. If you do not say it, who will?

EMPATHY AND INTERCONNECTEDNESS

Empathy is the ability to appreciate the feelings and perspectives of others. In the case of technology, empathy is represented by user-centered design. User-centered design articulates that technology resources should meet the needs of the user as much as possible, rather than the user adjusting his or her needs to fit what the technology can accomplish. As an example, many of America's classrooms are populated with awkward one-piece desk-chair combinations. These seats are neither comfortable nor adjustable to fit various students' frames. A more user-centered design might allow students to adjust the height of the pieces and to move the chair separately from the desk. User-centered design in technology can focus on either hardware (e.g., computer mice adjusted for the size of a child's hand or adjustable-height monitors) or software (such as Grolier's elementary-friendly interface that has larger fonts and removes the too-difficult *Encyclopedia Americana* from the search results).

Striving for user-centered design can mean sticking one's neck out. It can mean advocating for age-appropriate passwords for primary students, renaming printers so they are easily identified by the user, buying simple-to-operate cameras instead of ones with multiple dials, or selecting elegantly-designed software that feels more intuitive.

But empathy means something else as well. It means respecting the professionalism and expertise of colleagues, even those who are different from oneself. SLMSs have a responsibility to tread lightly and respectfully when dealing with all teachers and students. Different users interact differently with technology, and meeting users where they are preserves their dignity and respect. For example, some adults prefer that you purchase an extra copy of a manual so that they can learn privately; others prefer face-to-face support; others want a few links to YouTube videos that demonstrate the tool in use. Teachers are at different points on the technology competency continuum. It can be frustrating to invest time teaching someone how to upload an attachment when you would prefer designing online activities in a Moodle or Blackboard course. But just as teachers are being asked to differentiate their instructional methods and resources to meet a diverse student body, we must be patient and differentiate with our staff.

I wish I could say that this were easy. SLMSs are busy, and often these interactions take up a disproportionate amount of time. Try shifting lenses and asking what you can learn about that person or from that person during the transaction. As you sit together as a CD burns or as a photo uploads to an email account, you may discover that the colleague you are supporting has a great classroom management suggestion or can bring you an idea from a colleague at the other end of the building. Remember Jimmy Fallon's recurring role on *Saturday Night Live* as Nick Burns, the sarcastic computer guy who blamed the user for all problems before braying, "MOOVE!" and fixing the problem? (For a sample, visit http://www.nbc.com/Saturday_Night_Live/video/clips/nick-burns/2786/.) No one wants to work with Nick Burns!

Empathy is intrinsically linked with interdependence. Schools are unique environments where real success comes when the weight of the needs of everyone is balanced by everyone. Interdependence asks staff to lock hands instead of standing alone. As an SLMS, maintaining that fragile position can be difficult, especially when technology budgets are limited and it may not be possible to meet each person's request each year.

Interdependence leads us to consider whether to purchase a single license of premiere software or a site license of less expensive, less robust software that can be accessed on every computer in the building.

Interdependence is also about access; it is what urges us to follow the Common Belief of the AASL *Standards for the 21st-Century Learner* supporting equitable access, not only to technology but to information and rigorous learning (AASL 2007). Interdependence is what helps the SLMS keep track of the big picture so that all students and teachers have equal access.

Being part of an interconnected, district-wide supply chain in which the SLMS is in the middle between tech services and classroom practice requires tact and strong communication. Too often, this role of "go-between" is laden with stress. However, SLMSs have a responsibility to communicate the needs of each party. They are at the center of the inevitable priority struggles that arise: teachers' need for customization and intuitive interfaces and the tech department's need for network security and identical machines.

WALKING THE TIGHTROPE BETWEEN RESPONSIBLE INNOVATION AND FOOLISH RISK

SLMSs walk the line between embracing innovation responsibly and acting impulsively. External pressure comes from professional journals or fellow SLMSs to hop on the latest bandwagon and adopt the latest gadget. But today's innovation can quickly turn into tomorrow's reject. (Don't all libraries have a storeroom Corner of Shame where the wonder tools of the past—opaque projectors, old computer microphones, PalmPilots, two-megapixel cameras, and external floppy drives—reside?)

SLMSs rarely have extensive budgets and must make selections carefully, in consultation with the technical services department, classroom teachers, building leadership, and even students, in some cases. SLMSs may also need to weigh the overall tensions and stresses of the school building. Too much innovation, and overstressed teachers may tune out. Too little innovation, and the culture of continual growth and experimentation can weaken.

Luckily, in the Web 2.0 and Web 3.0 age, the amount of risk has shrunk considerably. The cost of technology tools continues to decrease, many Web-based tools are free, and many software options have a free downloadable trial. "Try before you buy" is a new reality that lets the SLMS make educated guesses, try out hunches, and enjoy the rush of trying something new. Doing so keeps returning us to the role of user and reminds us of our responsibility to keep the end-user (a teacher, staff member, or student) in mind when making decisions. Part of remaining a continuous learner is continuing to try new things, and part of being a leader is creating similar test-drive opportunities for staff and students.

Some educators lament the number of sites that are blocked and cannot be tried at school. Some districts have restrictive filtering policies that block sites such as YouTube, blogs, Google Docs, games (including educational games), and more. *It is too tempting to blame lack of personal growth on a district's filtering policy.* Try blocked tools at the public library (most do not filter their Web content) or at home. Having hands-on practice before appealing unblocking the site can bolster your case.

Balancing between innovation and risk is challenging. But it is part of the SLMS's responsibilities.

EMBRACING FLEXIBLE THINKING

In the past, technology was rigid, and the user had little input on how to use it. When my father was a building principal in the late 1970s and early 1980s, he introduced us to our first computers: black Apple II+ computers. They took just one kind of disk: 5-1/4″ floppies. They used just one kind of software and had no lowercase letters. They were not flexible technologies: they were take-it-or-leave-it technologies.

Today, however, there is a plethora of options. One can communicate learning with a PowerPoint or a podcast. One can share ideas via blog comments on Edublogs or Blogger or collaborate on a wiki from PBWorks, Wikispaces, or Wetpaint. Students can exchange quick messages via email, instant messaging, videoconferencing, or Twitter. Need information? Search on Google or one of a dozen other search engines, or create a custom search engine. Want visual content? Watch videos on YouTube or Vimeo, via iTunes or UnitedStreaming, on Hulu or via a network's Web site. The options are endless . . . and a new tool will be here tomorrow if today's is not effective.

This has been a gift to the SLMS. Rather than having to promote a single resource or tool as "the" choice, the SLMS can assemble a toolkit of technology options. This helps differentiate teaching and learning experiences, matching users with the "just right" tool. If you do not like Blogger, then try Edublogs. Need a collaborative platform? It could be Moodle or Wikispaces or Google Docs . . . or a combination. Similarly, students can be empowered to select technology tools and create products that best communicate their messages. Students are no longer corseted by what is available in the era when *everything* is available.

Being freed from having to hawk "the" purchased tool also lets the SLMS "lead with the need." It flips the tables. No longer do teachers have to use what is available; instead, teachers and students can collaborate with the SLMS to find the tool that meets an authentic teaching or learning need. Instead of humans serving the technology, technology serves the humans. It is the end of the "tools for tools' sake" era.

KEEPING THE "EDUCATIONAL" IN EDUCATIONAL TECHNOLOGY

A murmur is emerging from Library Land, and it has to do with how technology is used. SLMSs are beginning to share their concerns that they are seeing too much poor use of technology. The number one suspect: bad PowerPoint, where cut-and-pasted text and three bullet points whiz by, complete with sound effects and animations. Had the student turned in the text as a paper, the total output might have comprised 15 to 20 sentences at the most. But it is not merely the quantity of learned content that concerns the SLMS. The bullet points barely move beyond a regurgitation of facts; they demonstrate little synthesis or conceptual understanding. Judging from the glazed-over looks of the students in the audience, the class knows the project means little and does not merit their attention.

Alas, such a project may meet the objectives of a district's outmoded technology scope and sequence, one which prioritizes integration of various PowerPoint features: transitions, animations, graphics, and bullet points. The facts are certainly accurate (though they sound suspiciously like Wikipedia). A day was spent on research plus two weeks in the computer lab to create the PowerPoint. But is the project a success? No. What has the student learned? What has the student thought about and considered? What new understandings are present? Alas, none. What did the project end up demonstrating? With a heavy heart, you wonder if the project demonstrates little more than a student's ability to follow the directions on the PowerPoint tips sheet.

This scenario (adapted from Fontichiaro 2008) is unfortunately too familiar in America's schools. Some adults become so enamored with the visual appearance of the PowerPoint that they do not realize that little has been learned. How, with instructional time so limited, has it happened that so much time was wasted on so little learning?

As mentioned earlier in this chapter, the release of the refreshed NETS*S and AASL *Standards for the 21st-Century Learner* call on us to break away from brain-dead technologies. An SLMS who wants to be a technology leader is strategic about shepherding in changes in instructional practice that up the ante for student learning. Doing so means stepping outside the "quiet zone" of the library and finding opportunities to advocate for higher-quality learning experiences. We can request staff meeting time to discuss that merely *using* technology is not the goal any longer; using technology as a tool to support quality learning is the new objective.

Here are some questions that might be discussed at a staff meeting:

- How does [the technology tool] help students learn and/or express their new understandings?
- What new understandings will be demonstrated as a result?
- If we transferred this student's information into pencil-and-paper format (removing the bells and whistles), would we consider this to be quality work? If it is great work, what attributes demonstrate that excellence? If not, how can we improve it?
- How could we use time differently to maximize the number of hours spent learning inquiry, problem-solving, or critical thinking skills versus having time to "make things pretty"?
- Is this instructional design "outsourceable" to a country like India? How could we transform it so that the kind of critical thinking it would take to complete the project could only be done here to promote American innovation?
- Imagine that the student is going to a job interview. In his or her portfolio is the project under discussion. The interviewer asks, "What did you learn from this project that can contribute to our company?" How would your student answer?
- Is the current tool the best tool? Why? What new Web-based or software-based tools might be even more effective (that did not exist when this project was envisioned)?
- Are we helping students use technology effectively to speak to an authentic audience? How would bringing "audience" into the instructional conversation change the result?

These can be tough questions for everyone in a school setting, but technology leadership is more than hardware and software. Technology leadership in a school setting travels hand-in-hand with instructional leadership.

SAVING TIME FOR SELF-REFLECTION

The ability of the SLMS to reflect on what has happened is a powerful way to plan for the future. The day-to-day life of the SLMS is far busier than ever. Whether teaching, collaborating, circulating, repairing, shelving, rebooting, booktalking, planning, troubleshooting, unjamming, or supporting, it is understandable that some SLMSs merely want to go home and put their feet up at day's end. But to do so would be to cut oneself off from a far greater sense of satisfaction, one that can come through reflection. Carve out some time to reflect on what has been happening. What trends have you noticed? Which tools are no longer as motivating as they once were? What should go on the technology wish list? What does the tech services department need to know about a pattern of errors that has been emerging? What training do you need to move forward? What do the teachers need? What do the students need? How can parents be involved? Are students learning what they should be?

Reflection must be consciously slotted into practice. Some SLMSs find that revisiting their lesson plan book and notating how the lesson actually evolved can be useful. Some use passing time between classes to scribble a note. Others use their media center blog for public reflection. Some keep professional journals. Some use writing for publication as a pathway to reflection. Darling-Hammond (2008) points out that metacognition, or thinking about one's own thinking, is one of the three key components to meaningful student learning. As professionals, we can lose sight that it is also one of the three keys to *our* meaningful learning.

CONCLUSION

The *Lost in Austen* takeoff on *Pride and Prejudice* mentioned at the start of this chapter showed an age when a groom drove the horses while his master or mistress sat inside the carriage. It is easy for SLMSs to see themselves as the groom who is the leader of the carriage ride. The groom holds the reins, after all, which drive the horses onward. But such an answer is too simplistic. For the groom only has the reins because they have been granted to him by the passengers. SLMSs, as technology leaders, have precious passengers—students, staff, and administration—who have lent them the reins. Technology leadership, like carriage driving, is a team sport. It is only through empowering others' work—whether that be through creating a vision, acquiring necessary equipment or software, or jiggling the recalcitrant power plug—that we truly emerge as leaders.

Strange visions like this can enter one's mind when watching a Jane Austen DVD, but ultimately, there is a metaphor embedded there that seems to define technology leadership quite nicely. Being a leader means that the ultimate goal—in *Lost in Austen* it is getting the passengers to their destination, while at school it is using technology to maximize student learning—takes priority over who does what. Being a leader can mean designing the carriage, building the road, or being willing to kneel into the dirt and fix the broken wheel.

REFERENCES

American Association of School Librarians. 2007. *Standards for the 21st-century learner*. http://www.ala.org/aasl/standards (accessed June 24, 2009).

Andrews, Guy, and Jane Austen. 2008. *Lost in Austen*. DVD. Directed by Dan Zeff. Chatsworth, CA: Image Entertainment.

Blowers, Helene. 2006. Learning 2.0 professional development module. http://plcmcl2-about.blogspot.com/ (accessed June 23, 2009).

Costa, Art, and Bena Kallick. 2009. Habits of Mind. Web site. http://www.habitsofmind.net/ (accessed June 24, 2009).

Darling-Hammond, Linda. 2008. *Powerful learning: What we know about teaching for understanding*. San Francisco, CA: Jossey-Bass.

Economist.com. 2009. Kaizen. http://www.economist.com/businessfinance/management/displaystory.cfm?story_id=13480663 (accessed June 21, 2009).

Fontichiaro, Kristin. 2008a. A technology metamorphosis: Redefining how students interact with technology. *Media Spectrum* 35 (2): 15–17.

———. 2008b. *Podcasting at school*. Westport, CT: Libraries Unlimited.

———. 2009. Nudging toward inquiry: Re-envisioning existing research projects. *School Library Media Activities Monthly* 26 (1).

———. 2009. 21st-century learning in school libraries. Santa Barbara, CA: Libraries Unlimited, an imprint of ABC-CLIO.

Fontichiaro, Kristin, and Susan Ballard. 2009. A letter to our classroom colleagues. *Knowledge Quest* 37 (3): 80–82.

Gladwell, Malcolm. 2005. *Blink: The power of thinking without thinking*. New York: Little, Brown.

Harvey, Carl. 2009. For good. Library Ties. Blog. http://carl-harvey.com/libraryties/2009/06/06/for-good/ (accessed June 23, 2009).

International Society for Technology in Education. 2007. *National educational technology standards for students*. http://www.iste.org/nets (accessed June 24, 2009).

———. ISTE Second Life. http://www.iste.org/content/navigationmenu/membership/member_networking/iste_second_life.htm (accessed June 23, 2009).

Levitov, Deborah. 2007. One library media specialist's journey to understanding advocacy: A tale of transformation. *Knowledge Quest* 36 (1): 28–31.

Zmuda, Allison. 2007. Hitch your wagon to a mission statement. *School Library Media Activities Monthly* 24 (1): 24–26.

8

Staff Development—Teacher-Librarians as Learning Leaders

Janice Gilmore-See

Staff development, while it should not, often exists as a random event on a particular day of the school year, seemingly disconnected from the real work of the teaching staff. Teacher-librarians can become learning leaders in their schools and districts if they understand what the teaching staff needs and can help plan worthwhile experiences.

Professional development days, meant to allow teachers to stay current with changes related to teaching and learning, should be meaningful learning experiences, but many have evolved into dreaded but required events. School-wide and district-wide staff development varies in content and quality from fabulous to necessary, relevant to boring, informative to tortuous. Depending on the culture of the organization, there may be a single focus with all programs coming together to support one goal. In other cases, leadership will have a vague and ill-defined direction, grasping at every passing educational fad to solve perceived or even nonexistent problems.

Additionally, these training days are often mandated by the district or state, and the topic, time, and location are not aligned with teacher priorities. Sometimes all staff development days are lumped together the week before school begins, when teachers want to be in their classroom moving desks and prepping their rooms. Other times, staff development days are scattered throughout the school year, but the scheduling requires teachers to write plans for substitute teachers and be away from their classroom. When teachers are not interested in the topic, they may exhibit disengagement—grading papers, checking email, surfing the Internet, or worse, talking through the entire session. Teachers show their displeasure by showing up late, sneaking out early, and generally behaving in a manner they would never tolerate from their own students. Teacher-librarians can change this behavior and make staff development more meaningful when they adopt a leadership role . . .

UNIQUE ROLE OF TEACHER-LIBRARIANS

Teacher-librarians often exist in a special category of teachers. Teacher-librarians are not considered classroom teachers, yet they manage the biggest classroom in the school, one that serves not only the students but also teachers, parents, and sometimes the community. For the purposes of professional learning communities (PLCs), which will be discussed in depth later in this essay, they may not have a group of teachers to meet with on a regular basis even though they may be the catalyst for the development of PLCs. Principals often group teacher-librarians with other support staff: reading specialists, resource specialists, speech and language teachers, and counselors. As a support team, these teachers may be called on individually or as a group to any PLC to help with a specific instance or problem.

Effective teacher-librarians are constantly and consistently managing the many facets of their job competing for their time. In consultation with their principal or other administrator they can be a major force in planning staff development activities aligned with the mission of the school. Prioritizing and allotting their time becomes a necessary activity in performing their leadership role in the school. How much time is spent in direct service to students versus collaboration with teachers? Is there more attention given to preparation for scheduled class visits or in promoting free and open access to the library? Is there adequate time to manage the administrative aspects of the library and support the school's reading incentive program? Is the teacher-librarian expected to complete both the teacher aspects of the job and the clerical, shelving books and working the circulation desk? When is there time to learn new technologies and also attend all the meetings that are necessary to know what is happening in the school? Should the library open before school, remain open after school, or both? How much time can be spent preparing to deliver staff development to teachers versus managing the textbooks and teacher materials efficiently?

Inclusion of the people most directly affected by professional development enhances the content and improves the buy-in of teachers and acceptance of new approaches. Corcoran (1995) notes that school leaders can undermine the legitimacy and effectiveness of professional development by failing to include participants in planning and delivery.

Successful teacher-librarians are valuable because they have a clear understanding of the school and its needs. Classroom teachers focus on the issues in their classroom and in their PLC, but the teacher-librarian has a wider view of the school. In smaller schools, they are often the only staff member on campus who knows every single student, usually by name. Teacher-librarians can clear the pathway for teachers by providing staff development and procuring the tools, strategies, and access they need. They remove blockages by advocating for the needs of the whole school, not just specific teachers or students. The teacher-librarian is also the one who orders, manages, instructs, and promotes the use of these resources.

Teacher-librarians remain focused on the end result of school-wide student achievement and will not take "No" for an answer when they encounter obstacles. They often develop an exhaustive list of supportive concerns and contacts when looking for funding sources to provide the tools the school needs:

- District funds
- Parent-teacher organizations
- School site councils
- Grants
- Corporate sponsorships
- Community partnerships

What characteristics of teacher-librarians are necessary for them to step into the role as school staff developer? They must have strong interpersonal and communication skills. Public speaking can be learned and improved over time, and teacher-librarians often find that the more they do it the more comfortable they become. However, there is a big difference between being comfortable speaking to a group of students and standing in front of peers. Additionally, teacher-librarians must be enthusiastic about children and teens and about their schools. They must believe that every student is important, has potential, and can succeed. Teacher-librarians need to be persistent, assertive, and confident that they can and should make a difference for all members of the school community.

Additionally, there are some areas where the teacher-librarian must remain current:

- Skills, knowledge, and attitudes about the changing information infrastructure
- Standards and curriculum—specifically, the adopted texts and teacher materials, their organization and component pieces, and how they are used or meant to be used in the classroom
- Pedagogy
- Team building, team structures

So, then, how does a teacher-librarian help plan ongoing learning opportunities and support for the faculty? And how does this, in turn, translate to better results for students? One contemporary answer is through PLCs. These require knowledge of the concept and the ability to organize and lead the communities.

LEADING PROFESSIONAL LEARNING COMMUNITIES

Providing learning opportunities for professional educators is at the core of the PLC. Typically, teachers in a PLC meet on a regular basis in learning teams organized by grade level or content area assignments and share responsibility for their students' success (Darling-Hammond et al. 2009). These learning teams are committed to following a cycle of continuous improvement using the following eight-step process.

1. PLCs analyze student data

   - What are students expected to know based on applicable standards?
   - What do they already know? There is no use in teaching content that is already mastered.
   - Are students ready to learn the content? Is there background or foundational knowledge that is missing?

2. PLCs examine educator needs

   - Using the results of the student data, is there an area where additional educator learning is necessary?
   - Are there concepts or skills that are difficult to teach?
   - How are other successful educators doing it?
   - What do the experts say?

3. PLCs locate and participate in appropriate staff development opportunities

   - Is there someone on campus who already knows?
   - Is this something that all teachers need to learn or something specific to one teacher or a small group of teachers?
   - Who will attend the training? Where? When?

4. After attending staff development workshops, the educators apply what they've learned by practicing new strategies and developing powerful lessons

5. The PLC designs or acquires common assessments to measure student growth

   • Assessments should be embedded in the curriculum and not stand-alone instruments disconnected from student learning.
   • Multiple formative assessments should be given, not just cumulative and summative ones.

6. PLCs return to the students' formative results

   • How effective have the new strategies and lessons been?
   • Are there ways to fine-tune to make the learning even more effective?

7. PLCs reflect on their professional practice

   • How has it changed the impact on student learning?

8. PLCs repeat the cycle with new goals

PLCs offer opportunities and challenges for teacher-librarians and their role in the school. Teacher-librarians have a unique ability to serve as a site-based staff developer because they are available to teachers, administrators, and other school employees to coach and help them. The teacher-librarian can present new information, model a new strategy, or help problem-solve at staff meetings. Teacher-librarians can be available for smaller meetings (PLC, department, grade level, and the like), assist with designing and conducting action research, participate in seminars, coach one another, and plan lessons together with teachers.

Schools implementing the PLC model recognize that there are no quick and easy results. It is unlikely that a couple of days of professional development each year, or a few hours taken from prep periods, will change the culture of a school. How fortunate to have an on-site staff developer to reinforce all the learning! When new learning is introduced, consistent administrator encouragement teamed with a teacher-librarian's on-site support can help teachers as they implement and practice new learning, but the teachers must ultimately be the ones invested in the learning and committed to the process.

TEACHING TEACHERS: TEACHER-LIBRARIAN
AS LEARNING LEADER

Imagine that the principal announces, "We need one teacher who is willing to go and attend a staff development workshop and bring back the information to train us all in what this new program entails." Principals and district administrators often embrace the idea of sending one teacher to training who can return and become the trainer for the rest of the staff. There are advantages and disadvantages to sending a classroom teacher. The classroom teacher is appropriate when the training is meant to deepen and broaden knowledge of a particular content area or pedagogy of a particular discipline. However, there are many instances where the teacher-librarian is a natural fit.

When staff development is provided by the teacher-librarian, it can be site specific, designed for specific teacher groups, and allow sufficient time, support, and resources to enable teachers to master new content and to integrate this knowledge and skill into their practice.

- The teacher-librarian knows the school and its culture, including the students, the teachers, the parents, and the community.
- The teacher-librarian spends time staying current through professional reading and by the very nature of dealing with information and information technology.
- The teacher-librarian is able to provide just-in-time training.
- The teacher-librarian has no bias for content; structure, features, and format are stressed over "content-specific" knowledge. The teacher-librarian is not bound to content area, grade level, or department.

Teacher-librarians who serve as learning leaders are able to provide information in manageable chunks. This can be done for the whole staff or with specific groups. It can be done formally or informally because the library is accessible to all. It can be done during school hours or outside of the instructional day, but optimally, support is on-site and available at the time of need.

Knowing the audience is crucial. For example, if new technology is being introduced, some teachers are by nature early adopters. They may want a quick demonstration, followed by limited directions, some time to explore and play, and a chance to ask questions. It is tempting to format trainings for these early adopters, especially since they are the ones most likely to continue to use the information. "Innovation thrives when you find and encourage the right people. They return the favor by customizing and adjusting programs to match local needs, local people and local conditions" (McKenzie 1998). Thus, the teacher-librarian is instrumental in finding the other staff members who will learn, adopt, adapt, and spread the excitement to reluctant teachers.

The majority of teachers will need the staff developer to present a reason to learn, a "hook" that motivates them to try something new. Teacher-librarians must look critically at what is being presented and tap into the reasons that will entice teachers to want to learn. In addition, they really must know the staff and have worked over time to build trust. It may be helpful to consider the following questions.

- Will it save time?
- Is it a better way?
- Will it help students make progress?
- Will it work?
- Is there additional work involved, and if so, what is the payoff?
- Will it help teachers communicate with families, either to solicit assistance or to keep them informed?
- Will it help them by adding strategies for differentiating instruction for specific subgroups?
- Is it something teachers can employ as meaningful independent work for students?

TECHNOLOGY TRAINER

One leadership role that fits the teacher-librarian is that of technology trainer. Teacher-librarians are responsible for keeping up-to-date as new technologies evolve, and they purchase much of the software and hardware for the school's use. This places them in a logical position to teach, because the technology is in the library, and that is where teachers and students come to find answers. This is not easy, because one is teaching one's colleagues, not students.

Reluctant learners will want detailed, written instructions in simple language. Screen shots and other visual aids are helpful. Try a "dry run" of the training on a test group before standing up in front of the entire faculty. For some technology-resistant teachers, if it does not work the first time they will never try to accept it! Spend time anticipating potential problems and prepare materials to help teachers when they encounter those problems. What will you do if the product or application is incompatible with the teacher's computer? What programs must a teacher already have installed for the product to work correctly? For example, plug-ins such as Adobe Reader, Flash Player, Shockwave, Java, QuickTime, or Windows Media Player are often assumed.

Offer support over the long term—"You can email me or call me with questions and I will respond to you ASAP." This gives them the confidence to move forward rather than ignoring the training once the workshop is over.

Although it is tempting to go green, for training purposes you should have something in writing to give teachers. It can be brief. It should have space for teachers to take notes they can refer to during and after the training. Post the same information online as a PDF so teachers can find it in the future if they misplace their notes. Follow up after a short time to see what teachers learned and remember from the training. Ask for success stories or interesting things they found when using the new information. Ask teachers also what they dislike, and look for alternatives and workarounds.

If something about what they are using is less than optimal, do not start by apologizing and saying how bad it is. Explain, or better yet, show what the end result will look like and mean for their students, parents, or themselves. Then continue with the training.

A teacher-librarian may not be able to answer all questions, and it is best to confess ignorance if that is the case. If the question regards something important that everyone needs to know, the teacher-librarian can do the research and then share the answers. Sometimes it is not that the question cannot be answered but rather that the answer is best coming from a higher authority. For example, budget and policy decisions from the school board or principal may limit teachers' ability to access and use new tools.

PRACTICAL TIPS FOR TEACHER-LIBRARIANS
WHEN PRESENTING TO COLLEAGUES

1. Know the material inside and out. Tell teachers what they will learn and why it is important for them.
2. Be prepared and organized. Have handouts at the door so that participants can get them on their way into the room, or have them quickly at hand in the order needed. Passing things out takes time and stops the momentum of a presentation.
3. If using a presentation software program such as PowerPoint or Keynote, proofread it for misspellings or grammatical errors. When designing slides, remember that less is better:

   • Just put enough on the slide to guide the presentation
   • Use graphics instead of words if possible
   • Do not "read" the slide
   • Rule of thumb—no more than one slide per minute of the presentation

4. Practice the presentation until it flows easily. It does not have to be memorized. In fact, it is better if the wording is natural. Although it will sound a little bit different each time the

presentation is given, it is only important that all the key points are covered. It is a rare person that can stand up and give a stellar presentation without practice.

5. Be conscious of the time limit, especially if your presentation is part of a longer meeting. If it is a struggle to finish in time when practicing alone, the session is sure to go well over the allotted time when questions and disruptions occur. Also, if the training is supposed to fill a longer span of time, come prepared with extra material just in case things go faster than expected.

6. Have a back-up plan in case of technology failure:

   - What if the computer that holds the presentation fails? Bring the presentation on a thumb drive or post it online.
   - Does the presentation require Internet access? Think about preparing an alternate presentation with screenshots.
   - Does the presentation require the participants to have working computers? Consider what to do with participants who encounter technical difficulties or who show up without computers.

7. Make it safe for teachers to take risks when learning something new. Reassure them that there is nothing they can "break" if they do it wrong. Teachers are often afraid of looking stupid in front of their peers:

   - Ask participants to volunteer instead of calling on them.
   - If using an anecdote that includes someone known to the participants or someone in the room, get permission in advance before telling the story.

8. Do not criticize current or past practices. If the presentation takes teachers to task for something they are doing, or perhaps have done for years, there will be greater resistance to change.

9. Set behavior expectations for adult learners. Techniques that work with children can be used with adults as well. For example, proximity can discourage distracting side conversations. Give explicit instructions, for example, whether the audience should hold questions until the end or ask them at any time.

10. Solicit evaluations by providing a short form with at least one open-ended question. Use the feedback from your audience to improve presentations since this is the best chance to find out what worked and what did not.

Teacher-librarians become learning leaders in their schools and districts when they accept responsibility for helping plan staff development. They understand what the teaching staff needs to learn, and they have the ability to plan worthwhile experiences to meet their needs. By taking the lead, teacher-librarians make sure that staff development is more than a random event on a given day; instead, it will be development that is connected to the real work of the teaching staff.

REFERENCES

Corcoran, T. 1995. *Helping teachers teach well: Transforming professional development.* Research Brief No. 16-6/95. Philadelphia, PA: Consortium for Policy Research in Education.

Darling-Hammond, L., R. Chung Wei, A. Andree, N. Richardson, and S. Orphanos. 2009. *Professional learning in the learning profession: A status report on teacher development in the*

United States and abroad. National Staff Development Council. http://www.nsdc.org/news/NSDCstudy2009.pdf (accessed February 9, 2010).

McKenzie, J. 1998. Identifying and grooming the pioneers. *eSchool News.* http://staffdevelop.org/cadre.html (accessed February 9, 2010).

SUGGESTED READING

Borko, Hilda. 2004. Professional development and teacher learning: Mapping the terrain. *Educational Researcher* (33): 3–15.

Dufour, Richard, and Robert Eaker. 1998. *Professional learning communities at work: Best practices for enhancing student achievement.* Bloomington, IN: Solution Tree.

Fogarty, Robin, and Brian Pete. 2006. *From staff room to classroom: A guide for planning and coaching staff development.* Thousand Oaks, CA: Corwin.

Hord, Shirley, and William Sommers. 2007. *Leading professional learning communities: Voices from research and practice.* Thousand Oaks, CA: Corwin.

Jolly, Anne. 2008. *Team to teach: A facilitator's guide to professional learning teams.* National Staff Development Council.

9

Leadership and Your Professional School Library Association

Blanche Woolls

A professional school library association is made up of members with common interests. These members are the association, and their work within the association guarantees a common effort to improve the situation of school librarians and their libraries in the local area, the state, or the nation, depending upon the purview of the association. Many times one hears school librarians asking why their state association does not do something about an inequity in the treatment of school librarians, forgetting that they are the state association, and whatever the association does is what its members are able to accomplish. They represent and are responsible for their association and its activities, along with the mission, goals, and objectives. What "the association" can do is limited only by the ability of members to make things happen.

Some school librarians are lucky enough to be encouraged to become active in their professional associations as students in their credential programs. They join at the student membership rate and even attend a local or state association meeting. When a national meeting is held fairly close by and they can attend, they discover how much larger these are compared to state meetings. With graduation, reality sets in, with new jobs in schools where they must now pay dues for the teachers' association or union at the local, state, and national levels. On a beginning school librarian's pay, joining a second organization seems a luxury—if not at the state level, definitely at the national level. The longer one excuses oneself from this added expense, the less likely one will return to the more specialized professional experience later. This is unfortunate for all school librarians.

For those who continue membership in both the teachers' association and the school library association, networking begins with fellow librarians, learning what they are doing in their schools, how they are approaching problems that are often more prevalent than could be imagined. Many associations offer an online list where members can pose questions or concerns, ask for help analyzing failures, report successes, or keep in touch with one another. At professional meetings participants learn both what works and what does not work, and they can gather suggestions for different approaches to solve common problems. Programs at conferences address school library trends and issues as they relate to the wider picture of education in schools and to those who are working in school libraries, supervise school libraries within a district, or teach potential school librarians. Such librarians are making the commitment to serve as active members in the association, and they are also learning to be leaders.

TRAINING TO BE LEADERS

Associations provide opportunity for school librarians to learn and practice their leadership skills. Members who are elected to office in some associations are provided formal training in conducting meetings, following parliamentary procedure, organizing and leading groups, and meeting the media. In other associations, these things are learned through practice.

The good meeting leader must set an agenda, often with the assistance and consent of the group, and make sure that the meeting progresses in a timely fashion. Conducting the meeting means keeping the group focused on the agenda and skillfully returning to the agenda before any discussion gets too far from the topic. This is a skill that can be learned and practiced and put to good use in other situations.

Following parliamentary procedure is made much easier by getting a copy of the rules the organization has in place, whether Robert's or Sturgis's or another. If the association is very formal, many officers will be assisted by a parliamentarian, who helps with questions about the appropriateness of a motion, whether it has been seconded, what discussion may ensue, and when a vote is appropriate. While it is easier when a parliamentarian is available, leaders need to have some basic information to be able to work effectively with this person. When no parliamentarian is available, the officer must be very familiar with the rules, or it will be very difficult to have any meaningful progress at meetings toward accomplishing the goals of the association.

Officers in associations must be able to organize and lead groups. Sometimes this training is given as a part of the training a school librarian receives before being awarded his or her credentials. However, this is not standard across all certification programs; the school library association may also offer group dynamics as a part of the training for their officers and members. When these opportunities are offered, take the time for the training.

Training to lead groups can be useful for school librarians back at their schools. They must also learn how to make presentations to faculty; leading this group and beginning training in group dynamics is useful to prepare for collaboration with faculty. Also, knowing how to interpret body language of an audience is always helpful to being a successful presenter.

One other aspect of leadership that is most useful to officers and leaders within an association is training in how to meet and talk with the media. This is especially helpful if librarians in the school district are trying to deflect a censorship problem, fight for more funding for school libraries, or even promote a particularly successful program, such as a day when the local member of Congress pays a visit to the school and the media comes too.

Association officers and leaders learn how to speak in "sound bites" that resonate. If a school librarian is asked to be on a radio or television news broadcast, it is an excellent opportunity to promote the school library program in his or her building, the program across the district as a whole, and even the role of school libraries in the education of children in the state.

PLACES FOR LEADERSHIP PRACTICE IN ASSOCIATIONS

Associations usually have a wide variety of places to learn to exert leadership, beginning with those places where one introduces oneself to the organization in committee meetings and workshops. This could be a letter you write to the editor in response to an article in the association's publication. This may also be an article you would write and submit to your local newspaper.

Conferences of associations provide opportunities for members to hear outstanding speakers during the major sessions. They also provide the dais for members to tell smaller groups the good things that are going on in their schools and school libraries through poster sessions, which are panels with pictures and text explaining an activity. Sometimes an abstract of these sessions is published before the conference program. This is an excellent way to make a good impression and allows school librarians to practice presenting information to an audience; also, this audience may be less formidable than a larger group or than making a similar presentation to one's teachers and principal or board of education. It is an excellent training ground.

A participant can also work to become a member on a committee. Associations offer a wide variety of committee opportunities, and some of these are more sought after than others. It will be easier to get an appointment to a less popular committee than one that is considered a choice appointment.

Many associations have a governing body composed of members elected to serve in this larger group. If the association is made up of all types of librarians, school librarians are often reluctant to run, because they think that they will not be elected or that they will be elected but will not be able to attend the conferences to participate fully. Many associations are investigating alternative ways to participate, but at the present time, most members of association councils must pay all expenses to attend meetings, including registration fees, transportation, lodging, and meals at the conference. Such a commitment can be a detriment to running for a governing position, but school librarians must plan to do this so that their school librarian voices are heard. Some school districts will pay for this if they are convinced that having a faculty member on state and national committees and serving in offices is good public relations for the district.

Officers of associations are usually elected for a term of one year as officer-elect, a year as the officer, and then a year as a past-officer. This means you will be making a three-year commitment to the association unless the term of office is even longer. Effective officers must do their "homework," and this may be daunting to a school librarian with a day job.

By understanding the choices of possible leadership roles within an association, one begins the process of achieving such a role. One of the best ways to do this is to find a mentor to help you make the final choice and move forward.

FINDING A MENTOR

Your first opportunity to meet a mentor may be through your school librarian from when you were a student in elementary, middle, or high school. These persons are almost always delighted to be able to introduce you to fellow librarians.

Another person who is always happy to share good students with the greater world is the person in charge of the school library certification in your college program. Library educators seem to be better able to get time off to attend conferences, so they are present to introduce you, and they also like to show off their prize students.

Some associations ask members to volunteer to take a first attendee around the conference. This serves the purpose of helping you figure out the conference program and helping you choose the best things for you to do while you are at the conference.

If you have had the pleasure of working with a mentor, that person will be the logical person to introduce you to the power persons in the association. Knowing who is going to be making those appointments to committees, as well as meeting the chair and members of the nomination committee to express your interest in an active role, is more easily accomplished if you do have a mentor who is on the inside track, helping you to achieve your goal.

ACHIEVING YOUR ROLE IN ASSOCIATION LEADERSHIP

To move quickly into any working role in an association, your mentor can sponsor you simply because he or she will be able to tell you which committees are sought after and will probably have appointments made from longer-tenured members. If you have started your networking as a student, your professors may be able to help you choose what to ask and from whom to ask it.

All associations differ, and in some all appointments are made by the president. In others, a committee is named by the president to help fill committee positions. In many, someone who wishes to serve must fill out a form, and this form is turned into the person(s) making these appointments.

Committee chairpersons are often asked to suggest names to be appointed to the committee. When this is the case, your attendance as a visitor at committee meetings will signal that you are interested in the workings of the committee and would like to serve as a member. Your mentor may be able to introduce you to the committee chair and members and tell them why you are interested in the committee, or you may be asked to introduce yourself as a guest at the committee, and at that point you can state why you are there and what your qualifications are.

If you have no one to help you with pursuing membership in a committee, you need to get a list of the committees; their formal charges will tell you what each committee is supposed to be doing and will list the committee's present members and any specific requirements for membership on that committee. This information is usually published annually in a membership directory, which may be available online and in print or posted in a publication of the association. You will have both mailing and email addresses. You will be able to determine if there are open seats on the committee and can then send a letter of interest to the chair, detailing why you would like to be a member and what expertise you would have to offer.

WORKING AS A COMMITTEE MEMBER

When serving on a committee, begin by participating actively rather than being someone who only seems to sit at the table; also, remembering the importance of participating, add to the discussion in a meaningful way. Usually when it is time for a committee chair to retire from the committee, the person who appoints or assigns new chairs will ask the former chair for suggestions. When you have been an active participant with helpful suggestions to move the agenda forward, your chair is more likely to suggest your name for the position.

Once you have been appointed to a committee, your work really begins. This appointment means you have made a commitment to attend all meetings of the committee. For local and state associations, this means attendance at their conferences, so you have made a financial commitment to your committee membership. Some committees may also have conference calls in the interim, and you will need to have read all the information so you can respond to discussion during the conference call.

Committees may review mission statements or strategic plans, choose winners of honors, or review the proposed budget. They may also encourage new members to join, revise bylaws, or nominate persons to run for offices or a council of the association. They may also review new materials for special lists or choose books for the state-wide readers' choice contests. To share the challenges of offering conferences, committees take responsibility for programs and other activities there. When organizations have publications, most will have a publications committee. Other committees are assigned to help members take responsibility for meeting government officials and legislators, helping them understand the role of school libraries, while another committee will help members support intellectual freedom. For an organization to have a presence, it needs to carry out advocacy. Finally, with the new technologies available, joining the global society can be made easier through international relations efforts.

The membership committee is vital to the association and to the profession. It is imperative that all school librarians be aware of the activities of the association and the goals and objectives for the profession. The more members join and participate, the more voice school librarians will have in the wider education community. As a member of this committee, you would be selling association membership to your fellow school librarians who are not members. You may provide transportation to meetings, share information you have learned, and talk about how essential it is to help the association by joining.

Serving on the publications committee usually means you are listed on the magazine as an advisor to the publication. You may be reviewing articles submitted for the magazine, to say whether they are suitable as is for publication or whether they need revisions and, if so, what revisions. You may be in a good place to write articles, because you will be present at the discussions regarding what is needed for your journal or newsletter, and you can volunteer to write them.

When the association has an appointments committee, serving there allows you to help determine who should be assigned the various positions within the association. For this committee, you will need to be able to assess a résumé listing skills of your colleagues so that they are placed in appropriate positions. This committee may also be in charge of nominating officers for the ballot, or the nominations committee may be a separate committee.

To serve on a budget committee it is essential to be able to look at a proposed budget and compare to the previous year's to determine if sufficient funding is available to carry out the activities of the association. This is seldom easy and often means making cuts, which will be difficult and may cause anger in members not on this committee.

The bylaws committee reviews the constitution when necessary. This committee may recommend items for voting by the membership to change the bylaws. This committee is for someone who likes to pay attention to detail; also, these members must know the difference between bylaws and policy statements. This committee may also translate bylaws into policies for the association or determine if a policy is in conflict with a bylaw.

Conference planning committees are always interesting, because they help pick the speakers and programming for upcoming conferences. The president or vice president also oversees such decisions as part of his or her responsibilities. Planning committees may be responsible for maintaining the registration desk at the conference, for making sure speakers are introduced at sessions, for thanking speakers at the end of a session, and for giving the speaker a small token for speaking. Depending upon shuttle service and taxi arrangements, a conference committee person may be asked to collect a speaker at the airport. This can be especially entertaining if the speaker is a well-known person you would like to meet.

In most library associations, those committee members who review new materials to be placed on "recommended" lists or who choose candidates for readers' choice contests get to keep copies of these materials. For this reason, membership on such committees is highly sought after. An appointment to one of those may require patience. It is often necessary to build a reputation for hard work and excellence in order to be chosen.

A fundraising committee is often appointed, and persons on this committee will find themselves asking for funds. Sometimes the process may pit you against another organization to which you belong or even your local school district. If your personality is not one that allows you to be comfortable in this situation, this may be a leadership role you would prefer to pass to someone else.

Most associations have a legislation committee to help members learn about upcoming laws and appropriations that impact on school libraries. This committee will see that contacts are made with appropriate persons to ensure proper attention. This committee may present programming at conferences to prepare members for making such contacts through email, regular mail, or visits to offices to discuss relevant issues.

Associations may have both a legislation committee and an advocacy committee, or these may be rolled into a single committee. Advocacy committees are responsible for planning ways to get the association, its members, and school library programs recognized to as broad an audience as possible. They will develop materials to share so that each member can work toward more attention being paid to the role of school libraries in the lives of students and teachers.

Some associations have an international relations component, because school librarians worldwide will benefit from knowing school librarians in the United States, and U.S. librarians can learn from others in the global community. National associations may help facilitate exchanges between members so that this committee provides exciting possibilities.

While associations may have many committees other than the ones mentioned here, the keys to being a successful committee member are: fulfill your obligation by reading everything sent to you, make the decisions you are asked to make, and participate in discussions about these topics. Nothing is more annoying than committee members who do not do their homework. And in contrast, hardworking committee members and chairs can be singled out to run for an office.

It is most likely that your first opportunity to exert leadership in a school library association will be in a volunteer role. You will be spending your own funds to communicate with other members, although the Internet has made communication much easier and less expensive. However, you will be spending your time away from your job carrying out these assignments, so you will be using time that you will not spend with family or on other leisure time activities. Payback is not immediate for your volunteer efforts, so you must be patient, knowing that you are serving the profession for the long term.

WORKING AS AN OFFICER

Association officers make committee appointments, set agendas, conduct meetings, and serve as the "voice" for the association. As officer-elect, you may be responsible for planning a conference, finding a location, organizing speakers for major programs, and making sure auxiliary programs follow the theme of the conference; you are also responsible to make effective committee appointments to facilitate the work of the organization. This can take a great deal of time and effort. Different committees directly related to the conference will have been appointed—perhaps the most important is the local arrangements committee. A strong exhibits committee ensures that attendees have something beyond the program to draw them to that site.

When an association is large enough, paid staff may manage the association. In this case much of the conference planning as far as location, negotiating with hotels, and choices of food for events becomes the responsibility of the office staff.

One should always remember that it is an honor to be asked to run for any office in an association; one should not be overly disappointed if not elected. In most associations you can choose to run again, and even the first time you run, you begin to gain name recognition. Until that time, you will need to plan how to find and achieve your role in your association's leadership.

ATTENDING CONFERENCES

While many associations are moving much of their business into the virtual world, attendance at conferences continues to provide excellent networking opportunities and the ability to look at new products and equipment in the exhibit area. Many conferences are held during the academic year, and you will need to be able to state your case for attending if you are going to be able to attend. The first rule is never to ask if you can attend a conference. Your query should be, "Where are the forms I must complete to ask for funding to attend X conference?" You need to have ready the dates of the conference, the probable expenses related to attending, and a list of those activities you will attend at the conference and how they will help you when you return to your school. If you just ask if you can attend and the answer is "No," then you are stymied unless you want to ask for a personal day off. At the higher level the principal or superintendent could placate you by saying, "We will only cover registration and your substitute," or any other piece or part of your request.

If you can get accepted to do a program for a conference that you want to attend, you may be in a much better position to ask for permission to attend from your administrator. As you are proposing a presentation for a conference, do not forget that if a teacher or administrator has been actively involved in the program you are presenting, having them come along with you allows them to participate in the conference and learn what is going on in other districts. Also, they can see exhibits of things you need in your school. Make an effort to nominate teachers and administrators for awards given by the association to honor other professionals or collaborative projects. As you and the teacher or administrator walk through the exhibits, he or she will see how new furniture would make the library a more attractive place for students. He or she can also see the new materials available to purchase. This is that picture that is better than a thousand words. The number of new books being published that would fit right into your curriculum will be overwhelming, especially if you have had very little budget for books over time. This opportunity also allows testing of databases for their use in the school. If your administrator or teacher goes back to the school with all these useful items in mind, they will be able to support your request for additional funds.

Whether or not conference expenses are covered, make sure you make a report of the sessions attended, the information learned, and anything else that will confirm the value of going to the conference. Such a letter can be sent to the principal with copies going to the superintendent and board. It is also always a good idea to scour the exhibit floor for posters and other things to bring back and share with individuals, at that moment or at a later time—perhaps to award as prizes for attending a staff development workshop you have presented or to give to students as reading incentives. Do not forget to mention to the administrator where these things came from, and be sure to sign up for every give-away while at the conference. You may win something wonderful for the library—another thing to tell that administrator.

LEGISLATIVE EFFORTS OF ASSOCIATIONS

Beyond the efforts of a committee within an association, many state associations have a strong lobbying arm and even hire their own lobbyists to support school library issues. This is still only a small beginning. That person, even the best lobbyist in the world, needs help. Members of the association must do their own part in the local area as well as the state. To do this, each member should make an effort to visit both state and national legislators in their home offices. To make this very easy, make an appointment to share some of the activities going on in the local school. Some school librarians, with the help of the principal, even invite their legislators to visit their schools, making a public relations event for all.

If you were to ask what does your professional association do for you, you would get a list of benefits such as networking, learning about issues facing school librarians, lobbying for school libraries, a venue for learning new techniques, and a list to help with quick solutions to problems.

You may turn this around, as President John F. Kennedy did, by asking what you can do for your association. By being a steady member, participating in association activities, serving on committees, attending conferences, writing for the association publications, and even taking on a position as an officer in the association, you are supporting school librarians and school librarianship. You are one of the members with common interests who guarantees a common effort to improve the situation of school librarians and their libraries, in the local area, in the state, in the nation, and perhaps even internationally. You are doing something about the inequitable treatment of school librarians, and you are introducing the world to the value of the school library in the education of students.

The definition of leadership as exhibited in the context of a professional association includes serving as an elected or appointed officer. You will be leading a committee or perhaps the entire membership to whatever is possible to improve the situation for school librarians everywhere. You are encouraging your association to move beyond planning an annual conference, offering a newsletter, or doing other things that organizations typically do. You will be leading when you lead the members of the association in setting an example in their libraries for what is an effective school librarian. You will be leading when you and others advocate for school libraries. You will be leading when you demonstrate the value of the school library in the education of students.

REFERENCES

Robert, Henry M., et al. 2004. *Robert's rules of order, newly revised, in brief.* Cambridge, MA: Da Capo Press.

Sturgis, Alice. 2001. *The standard code of parliamentary procedure* (4th ed.). Revised by the American Institute of Parliamentarians. New York: McGraw-Hill.

SUGGESTED MEMBERSHIP ASSOCIATIONS

American Federation of Teachers (AFT): http://www.aft.org/

American Library Association (ALA) and its divisions: http://www.ala.org/

American Association of School Librarians (AASL): http://www.aasl.org/

Association for Educational Communications and Technology (AECT): http://www.aect.org/

Association for Supervision and Curriculum Development (ASCD): http://www.ascd.org/

International Society for Technology in Education (ISTE): http://www.iste.org/

National Education Association (NEA): http://www.nea.org/

10

Shifting Our Vision for Our Futures: Leadership as a Foundational Element for Teacher-Librarians

David V. Loertscher

If one asks Google to define the term "leader," one of the interesting ideas that emerges is the following: "a person who rules or guides or inspires others." Notice that the three main words, "rules," "guides," and "inspires," are given equal billing, and if applied to a teacher-librarian or another specialist in the school who is not designated as the organizational boss, they seem at first to be contradictory. Yet, if we change the definition slightly to the idea that power ("rules") is a result of guiding and inspiration, this juxtaposition takes on enormous significance.

The presumption by many is that the position of teacher-librarian in a school is a relatively powerless position; yet, the same view is contradicted by the idea that information is power, knowledge is power, and wisdom is extremely powerful. Such a stereotype comes from the idea that the container of information, including the vehicle of delivery, is not important. That is, the telephone itself is not the important idea; rather it is the content of the messages delivered. It is not the keeper of the information or the conveyance that is paramount; it is the data and information delivered that are the primary concern.

For a half century, the position of teacher-librarian has been viewed by those both inside and outside the library profession as a selector and disseminator of information via the various popular devices at hand: a room where stuff is housed, managed, circulated, and maintained. Over this time, the vehicles have changed. Consider the evolution of the book itself, accompanied by a vast array of audiovisual devices and the emergence of the ubiquitous digital devices.

When we centralized the containers of information a half century ago, the librarians held power because we were the sole source of information and the devices needed to use that information. We held the keys to the treasury. Cross us at your own peril.

Three factors changed the landscape: the transfer of analog to digital, the appearance of the ubiquitous computing device, and the appearance of Google. Thus, in the last decade or so, a revolution of global significance has occurred: the democratization of devices, channels, and the information itself. Suddenly, I did not have to get out of my seat, walk down the hall, and enter the kingdom of the library. The library down the hall became a very minor information source as compared with the Internet; and, a vast and even overpowering information source was at my fingertips.

For those in our profession who presumed that the source of our power was the things and stuff we assembled and disseminated, the abrupt change has been disturbing. We have put up protective measures and arguments. Tradition, tradition, tradition has been the cry. The goal has been to try to legislate our position and force everyone into the tyranny of the past. It is not working and it will not work.

From whence does our leadership power emerge? Is it the stuff? The management of devices and delivery systems? The protection of things? From being the autocrat of a designated space? Sadly, our profession is split on this idea. I would pose the idea that it has never been about the stuff! If one reads and re-reads the various standards and professional literature across decades, it has always been about the use of information rather than its existence that mattered most.

For many, the power of the position as teacher-librarian came primarily from the transformation of things and resources into high-quality teaching and learning. Only secondarily did we rejoice in the means to the end.

We cannot fight, nor should we try to fight, the democratization of information and technology. It is a battle that has already been lost and was not our central role in the first place. The transfer of leadership power has already occurred. The sooner we transfer our source of power from things to the quality of teaching and learning, the better. It is not about the books. It is about the percentage of successful readers and lifelong readers. It is not about the information skills themselves; it is about the production of successful inquirers. It is not about the gathering of facts; it is about stimulating deep understanding.

All fields confront the same dilemmas in the era of ubiquitous information and information devices. Do we need doctors in the face of an onslaught of medical information at the fingertips? Do we need lawyers when the means of conducting legal business is freely available? Do we need athletic coaches or art teachers when the means to teach ourselves is readily available 24/7/365? Do we need teachers when the means of international delivery of instruction is possible?

Financial pressures and just plain ignorance have led to the question "Do we really need a library anymore?" The question arises when the assumption by both administrators and teachers is that stuff and devices were the central role of the library. Perhaps the enemy has been us all along. If we misinterpreted the source of our own power as things rather than enhancement of teaching and learning, then we must bear the burden of that misconception.

It is ironic in the face of conflicting information about the need for mammography at various ages that the advice is to "talk it over with your doctor." Yet, in the face of ubiquitous information and conflicting information, we do not hear the entire media community telling us to "consult your information professional." We already know that to just plug it in and turn it on in the world of technology does not automatically make a difference in how teachers teach, how kids learn, and how the results are achieved. So, why should we retreat as a profession? We should not retreat.

It is fascinating that a parallel example is sitting right under our noses. Most school districts hired tech directors to manage both administrative and instructional computing. Taking our Google definition to heart, many tech directors assumed that their power came from ruling rather than from guiding and inspiring. Suddenly, teacher-librarians discovered the problems associated with network dictators who were exacting organizational rules akin to centralized library rules. No. Do not. Cannot. Only on my timetable, not yours. Teacher-librarians are at the forefront of protest as access to information on any personal device becomes central to teaching and learning. Have we been hypocrites? Our message may have been: "You open your networks, but we prefer to keep control of our kingdoms!" We all need to realize that centralized control is neither desirable nor possible. Kids already know how to get around locked networks. They also know how to get around the school library to get what they need.

Just like doctors, we need not concern ourselves with ruling over medical information or, in our case, the world of information; rather, we transfer our leadership power to guidance and inspiration, and we make ourselves as indispensible as doctors are. To do this requires rethinking, critical thinking, creative thinking, and sound decision making on our part. We cannot presume that what we learned in library school still applies. We have to question everything we have always done.

Happily, the sources of information we need to shift our own focus sit right under our noses:

- We have the means to understand the trends across the nation in education and the various disciplines of teaching.
- We see a parade of teaching strategies marching through our libraries week in and week out. This gives us a perspective on the quality of teaching that few others have in the school.
- We watch as children and teens struggle with information and technology as the new digital generation. Few others in the school see the range of student behavior that we see.

In other words, the transfer of our leadership foundation comes from the data streaming into our heads, if we will only pay close and analytical attention to it and respond in thoughtful ways. It is upon that foundation that we build a vision that will not just confront the present but one that has sustainability over time. We cannot shift to being guides-on-the-side and inspirers unless our own vision shifts.

Many in the profession have already shifted the source of their leadership power and others are in transition. Still others try to ignore the fact that their house is built on the beach and the hurricane is moving at a steady pace toward them. I see great hope in the behavior of the leaders in our profession. Here are a few examples:

- A growing number are transforming their libraries into learning commons where the ownership is passed from the librarian to the teachers and students.
- Library Web sites, formerly one-way streams of information, are becoming more conversational and Wikipedia-like.
- School improvement is being centered in the learning commons as the idea of experimentation, action research, trial and error, and change is centered in this neutral territory of the school.
- Teacher assignments are becoming conversations rather than dictates. Students, teacher-librarians, teacher technologists, reading specialists, and other specialists enter the conversation, and inquiry rather than regurgitation becomes central.
- Library skills are being replaced with twenty-first-century skills. And, these skills are recognized as means to an end rather than ends in and of themselves. The skills drive deep understanding of content even when that content knowledge is shifting. The idea is that we are smart and flexible. We make decisions based on the best information at our disposal and can shift those decisions as knowledge evolves.

- The emphasis of technology is not upon the devices, networks, and the flashy Web 2.0 tools themselves but upon their impact as learning objectives and challenges are faced. Technology is the slave of learning; learning is not the slave of technology.
- The packaging and delivery of information is not as important as the impact of those systems on teaching and learning. If everyone in the school could now read the latest blockbuster novel, then it is my duty to see that everyone can access that resource whether in print, digitally, or via audio.
- Collaboration and co-teaching of learning experiences is still a foundational mission of the learning commons. "Bird" units and parallel teaching are not a part of the learning commons programmatic thrust.
- The teacher-librarian sits at the table of the central governance of the school and, in particular, the councils that are pushing curriculum, innovation, and achievement.
- The physical space of the learning commons has the look and feel of a learning space rather than a storage space.
- The various network systems operate seamlessly on whatever a teacher or student has as their preferred access device.
- The learning commons is the center of school culture both in physical and virtual space. Everyone has a sense of ownership and wants to contribute to the "commons" concept. We all build, construct, contribute, help maintain, and learn to act responsibly, ethically, and safely. There is a predominant atmosphere of "You help me; I help you; and, we all help each other."

There has been no more exciting time in the history of school libraries. Those on the carousel, however, have to reach out to capture the brass ring. Those who fail to shift their vision are already at risk of losing their positions. Industries that refuse to change, doctors who do not keep up, and individuals who do not keep retooling themselves are doomed. It is scary for some but the era of opportunity for others. It is the time to forge a powerful leadership position.

Index

About the Editor and Contributors

Doug Achterman has been an educator for 25 years and a library media specialist since 1998. He has written for numerous publications, including *School Library Journal*, *Teacher Librarian*, and *Knowledge Quest*, and his doctoral dissertation, "Haves, Halves and Have-Nots: School Libraries and Student Achievement in California" (University of North Texas, 2008) documents the positive impact school library programs have in that state. Doug was presented with the California School Library Association's President's Award for outstanding library media teacher in 2008 and has been honored with outstanding alumni awards at San José State University and the University of North Texas.

Helen R. Adams, a former Wisconsin school librarian with 30 years' experience, is currently an online instructor for Mansfield University, teaching "Access and Legal Issues," a class which encompasses First Amendment and intellectual freedom topics. She serves on the American Library Association Intellectual Freedom Committee, is the American Association of School Librarians representative to the Freedom to Read Foundation, chairs the Wisconsin Library Association Intellectual Freedom Round Table, and is a past chair of the American Association of School Librarians' Intellectual Freedom Committee. A frequent conference presenter, she is author of *Ensuring Intellectual Freedom and Access to Information in the School Library Media Program* (Libraries Unlimited, 2008) and co-author of *Privacy in the 21st Century: Issues for Public, School, and Academic Libraries* (Libraries Unlimited, 2005). She also writes a monthly column, "Intellectual Freedom Matters," for *School Library Monthly*. Helen lives on a tree farm in Wisconsin with her husband and German shepherd, Jake.

Sharon Coatney was a school librarian and teacher in Kansas for 30 years. Her school district was twice a recipient of the National School Library Media Program of the Year Award. She is a past president of the Kansas Association of School Librarians and the American Association of School Librarians, is a former councilor-at-large of the American Library Association, and was chair of the Standards Writing Committee for School Library Media, National Board for Professional Teaching Standards. Currently, Sharon authors a column about leadership for *School Library Monthly* and is the senior acquisitions editor for school library media for Libraries Unlimited, a division of ABC-CLIO.

Kristin Fontichiaro is an elementary media specialist and staff development facilitator with the Birmingham (Michigan) Public Schools and an adjunct lecturer at the University of Michigan–Ann Arbor. A member of the inaugural (2007) class of the American Library Association's Emerging Leaders program, Kristin was named the 2008 Distinguished Alumna of the Wayne State University School of Information and Library Science. Most recently, she edited *21st-Century Learning in School Libraries* (Libraries Unlimited, 2009). She is the author of *Podcasting at School* (Libraries Unlimited, 2008) and *Active Learning through Drama, Podcasting, and Puppetry* (Libraries Unlimited, 2007) and co-author, with Sandy Buczynski, of *Story Starters and Science Notebooking: Developing Student Thinking through Literacy and Inquiry* (Teacher Ideas Press, 2009). Her picture book *The Mitten* is forthcoming, as is an informational text for middle grade readers about podcasting. Her first informational text for children, *Go Straight to the Source!*, on primary source analysis, was published in November 2009 by Cherry Lake Publishing.

Janice Gilmore-See is a teacher-librarian and currently holds the position of district librarian for the La Mesa-Spring Valley School District. In that capacity, she provides professional development on a wide variety of topics to teachers and paraprofessionals. She is presently an officer in the California School Library Association. She holds a bachelor's degree in business, information systems, and a master's degree in library and information science from San José State University. She has written articles for *School Library Media Activities Monthly*, now *School Library Monthly*.

Violet H. Harada is a professor of library and information science in the Department of Information and Computer Sciences at the University of Hawaii at Manoa. In addition to her teaching duties, she coordinates the school library specialization for the Library and Information Science Graduate Program. She has published numerous articles in scholarly and popular professional journals on inquiry-based approaches to information seeking and use and on assessment strategies for student learning. Harada is a frequent speaker at state, national, and international conferences. She is the co-author of the following books: *Inquiry Learning through Librarian-Teacher Partnerships* (2004), *Assessing Learning: Librarians and Teachers as Partners* (Libraries Unlimited, 2005), *School Reform and the School Library Media Specialist* (Libraries Unlimited, 2007), *Collaborating for Project-Based Learning in Grades 9–12* (Linworth, 2008), and *Librarians as Learning Specialists: Meeting the Learning Imperative for the 21st Century* (Libraries Unlimited, 2008).

Ken Haycock is professor and director at the San José School of Library and Information Science, where he teaches and conducts research in leadership, governance, and role clarification. He is a past president of the American Association of School Librarians and of the Canadian School Library Association, as well as past member of the Executive Board of the American Library Association and past president of the Canadian Library Association. He is also past president of the Association for Library and Information

Science Education. The recipient of numerous awards for research, teaching, and service, Dr. Haycock holds a master's of business administration, a master's degree in education, and AMLS. His doctorate is in educational leadership and administration.

Jody K. Howard is an adjunct professor at the University of Denver, College of Education, Library and Information Science program, where she teachers a variety of classes including school library administration and collection management. Prior to teaching at the University of Denver, Jody was the manager of the School Library Masters and Endorsement Program at the University of Colorado at Denver. Jody also has experience as a classroom teacher, as a school librarian for grades K–12, and as a district library coordinator in a suburban school district in the Denver, Colorado area. In addition, Jody is a library consultant through her company, Creative Information Solutions for Library Organizations (CISFLO).

Deb Levitov is the managing editor of *School Library Monthly* (formerly *School Library Media Activities Monthly*) and *Crinkles* magazines. She worked for Lincoln Public Schools in Lincoln, Nebraska for 25 years as a school librarian, educator, and library administrator. She is the coordinator for the revision of the *Guide for Developing and Evaluating School Library Media Programs* (2000) by the Nebraska Educational Media Association (Libraries Unlimited, forthcoming). Starting in 2005, she has published the column "The Advocate" in *School Library Monthly*—providing examples of advocacy for school libraries by school librarians. She is a presenter for the American Association of School Librarians' Advocacy Institute, giving presentations across the country. She served for many years as the chair of the American Association of School Librarians' Advocacy @ your library® committee and chair and member of the American Association of School Librarians Advocacy Committee. She is currently a member of Camila Alire's Presidential Leadership Task Force for advocacy for the American Library Association. The topic of her dissertation was related to advocacy for school administrators.

David V. Loertscher is a past president of the American Association of School Librarians. He is currently a professor in the School of Library and Information Science at San José State University and serves as co-editor of *Teacher Librarian*. With two other professors, he organized the Treasure Mountain Research Retreat, held every two years with practitioners and faculty members discussing agendas for research and publication. His company, Hi Willow Research and Publishing, has been producing materials for school librarians for more than 30 years. He is a visionary who looks not at what was or is, but what should be and how it can happen.

Blanche Woolls has been a member of the American Association of School Librarians for 40 years. She has served as president of the American Association of School Librarians and as president of the International Association of School Librarianship, and she has consulted and spoken at conferences in more than 30 countries. She directed the School Library Certification program at the University of Pittsburgh for 25 years before becoming director of the School of Library and Information Science at San José State University. Since being named professor and director emeritus, she continues to teach in that program and is a consulting editor for Libraries Unlimited.